AN EXTRAVAGANZA OF STOOGE PHOTOS, PUZZLES, TRIVIA, COLLECTIBLES *AND MORE.*

STOOGE MANIA

TOM HANSEN
WITH JEFFREY FORRESTER

Illustrations by Tom Hansen

CONTEMPORARY
BOOKS, INC.
CHICAGO

Library of Congress Cataloging in Publication Data

Hansen, Tom.
    Stoogemania.

    Includes index.
    1. Three Stooges films—Collectibles.   2. Three
Stooges (Comedy Team)—Collectibles.   I. Forrester,
Jeffrey.   II. Title.
PH1995.9.T5H36   1984   791.43'75   84-21361
    ISBN 0-8092-5382-8 (pbk.)

Published by Contemporary Books, Inc.
180 North Michigan Avenue, Chicago, Illinois 60601
Manufactured in the United States of America
Library of Congress Catalog Card Number: 84-21361
International Standard Book Number: 0-8092-5382-8

Published simultaneously in Canada by Beaverbooks, Ltd.
195 Allstate Parkway, Valleywood Business Park
Markham, Ontario L3R 4T8 Canada

CONTENTS

ACKNOWLEDGMENTS

The authors wish to thank the following for assisting us in assembling this book:

John A. Barbour	Edward McCullough
Bob Baron	Barry Meister
Edward Bernds	Kevin Miller
Jim Corboy	Lisa Patterman
Gary Deeb	Peter Quinn
Robert Dempster	Dean Richards
Moe Feinberg	Bill Rosman
Bob Frischman	Anne Schwartz
Jack Getz	Barney Schwartz
Mark S. Gilman, Jr.	Eddie Schwartz
Nancy Gilman	Larry Sirotkin
Dick Hakins	Emil Sitka
Lori Hansen	Ray Smith
Donald Jacka	Dave Stuckey
Scott A. Kracen	Chuck Swirsky
David Maska	Greg Wilkin

Special thanks to Steve Cox for his eager assistance in pestering Stooge fans nationwide.

Moe, Larry, and Curly upon discovering their yearly salary matches
Abbott and Costello's laundry tab.

PREFACE

Stoogemania is a tribute—a celebration—of the Stooge phenomenon, the remarkable effect the Three Stooges comedy team has had on audiences worldwide. By now we're all familiar with their trademarks—the outrageous dialogue, bone-cracking violence, side-splitting dilemmas. And the lives of these performers—Moe, Larry, Curly, Shemp, Joe, and Curly Joe—have been chronicled in books and articles and on film. But *Stoogemania* goes beyond the theater, beyond the living room television set, into the marketplace and the lives of fans who have kept the memory of the team alive and are now celebrating a greater success story than even the Stooges themselves could have imagined.

The Three Stooges have affected our lives in virtually every area, from what we eat to what we wear, from 10-cent comic books to 100-dollar lithographs. And now they've even hit the pop music charts. *Stoogemania* celebrates the great influence the Stooges have had on contemporary culture.

Putting this book together wasn't easy. We're grateful to fans across the country who have opened their collections to us and shared their insights, anecdotes, and favorite collectibles. It's just that willingness on the part of the fans to share their affection for the Stooges that forms the backbone of this book. It's a fan's celebration, sharing in the fun and mayhem that prompted the Stooges to enter show business in the first place.

Read *Stoogemania* with an attitude of fun. And remember, we're all "victims of soicumstance!"

USING STOOGEMANIA

Many of the collectibles featured throughout this book can be found in shops, at antique shows, and from private collectors across the country. Where possible, we've tried to give you an idea of what some of the Stooge items are worth—or at least what collectors are asking for today. And we've listed many of the more accessible items in checklist form—catalog your collection by checking off items as they are acquired.

You'll also find a helpful section at the back of the book listing dealers and memorabilia shops that carry—or have access to—many of the Stooges items described here. And in most cases, they'd be happy to direct you to the right place if they don't have what you're looking for.

But keep in mind that many of the older Stooges collectibles are scarce or one of a kind. Happy Stooging!

INTRODUCTION

What is it about the Three Stooges that has made them the most talked-about comedy team in America today? From their beginnings in vaudeville (as actual stooges to Ted Healy's lead) in the 1920s to their success on television in the 1950s (and now in the 1980s as well), the Stooges relied on broad physical humor and split-second timing to entertain audiences. "Our comedy is based on upsetting dignity," Moe Howard once recalled, trying to explain the team's success with audiences and failure with the critics of their day. And now, after some 50 years, the Stooges have never been more popular.

Who were these guys, anyway? The Three Stooges were actually six Stooges. Moe Howard, the team leader and sometime manager, and Larry Fine, the middleman of the bunch, were the only constant members. The third Stooge was played by, in order, Shemp Howard, Curly Howard—both brothers to Moe—Shemp again (after Curly's untimely fall to a stroke), Joe Besser, and Curly Joe DeRita. They weren't artists, like Chaplin or Keaton. And any one of them would have told you that. Their films were

hastily constructed, at a pace that only today's weekly television actors could appreciate. They were largely ignored by the critics, and only two Stooges—Joes Besser and DeRita, the only living team members today—have witnessed the mass adulation and appreciation displayed by fans over the last few years.

So how has the team endured? And why are fans still enjoying these films produced some 50 years ago? Because the Stooges knew what was funny. They understood the common element, the thoughts of the guy on the street. Who hasn't, at one time or another, wanted to turn tail and run down the street to escape the tax man, the irate husband, a seltzer-bearing bruiser? The Stooges did it. Throughout their career, they invented comedy that reflected the desperation—and indignities—of real life.

It's ironic that the greatest Stooge success has come some four decades after the height of their film career, that fans across the country celebrate the Stooges, collectively and individually, long after the most heralded team members are gone. It wasn't always this way. The bulk of the Stooges' career was spent

1

A tired group of Stooges undergoes the rigors of publicity
photography. Such sessions were generally held at the end of a long
day's filming.

dodging barbs and brickbats—when they got any reaction at all—from film critics who acknowledged the team's humor but shook their heads at the Stooges' vehicle: the two-reel comedies, sometimes as many as nine a year. It wasn't until the mid-1970s that the Stooges' legacy hit its stride. A new generation of fans discovered the Stooges—on television—kids who had never read the criticism, who had never heard the PTA scream about the "violent influence" the Stooges' films had on young viewers. These new fans watched the Stooges because they were funny. Period.

Stooges films (the good ones, anyway) are simple, highly visual, and laced with the kind of wonderful dialogue that often hides the real humor until after you've heard the lines a few times. These shorts were not made to be analyzed, and that's precisely why they remain so popular today on television. So they didn't win an Oscar. They top the TV ratings in major cities and pack the houses at film festivals. And most importantly, the affection of their fans is legion. And after 50 years, who could ask for more?

COLLECTING THE STOOGES

Although their career began in the early 1920s, the Stooges enjoyed no real marketing success until the late 1950s. A lot of that had to do with the time period; there simply was no real effort to capitalize on the team's popularity, save the occasional giveaway item or publicity photo. But the volume of Stooges film work generated scores of truly collectible items, from stills, posters, and lobby cards to actual scripts from the films themselves. And by the time audiences discovered the Stooges on television, television had discovered marketing. A flood of Stooges material was released, from board games to T-shirts and virtually everything imaginable in between.

The value of Stooges collectibles varies greatly, depending largely on the scarcity of the item, the year it was produced, and the popularity of the Stooges trio it represents. Curly items are the most popular and demand the greatest price. Many of the film-related collectibles are hard to find, especially early movie posters. Some items, like Stooges T-shirts, are still being produced today.

Most of the prices quoted in *Stoogemania* are for items in mint condition (showing little or no signs of wear, all parts intact) and are the prices generally demanded by collectors and film buffs around the country. Dealers and retailers listed in this book generally can supply you with the Stooges merchandise described; many of the items are one of a kind, though, and may be difficult to locate.

Poster for *Gold Raiders*, a United Artists feature film with Moe, Larry, and Shemp. This poster is a rarity because *Gold Raiders* is the only feature that included Shemp as one of the Three Stooges.

MOVIE POSTERS

The Stooges appeared in more than 200 films. And each of those films was distributed to theaters with an advertising poster produced by the studio for promotional purposes. Unfortunately, many of the early posters have been lost; nobody really believed they'd be worth anything in those days, and consequently few have been saved. The posters vary in size from the standard one-sheet to the giant six-foot versions released for major feature films. The posters were, in most cases, issued to partici-

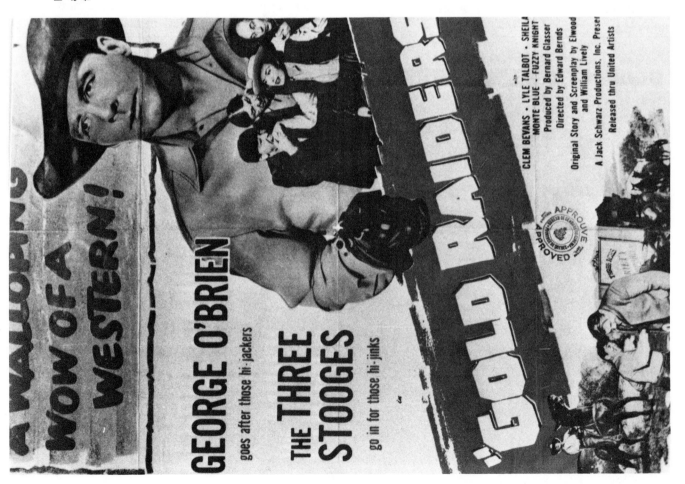

pating theaters free of charge, with the stipulation that they be destroyed upon completion of the booking. The few that remain are most likely part of an enterprising—and garbage-picking—fan's collection or leftovers from the studios' publicity department files.

Value

When you can find one, the early Columbia posters—*Woman Haters, Punch Drunks, Men in Black*—are among the most valuable, first, because they mark the beginning of the Stooges' starring career, and second, because they are so rarely seen. You can expect to pay $300–500, depending on condition. There are earlier posters, issued by MGM for various feature films the Stooges appeared in, such as *Dancing Lady* and *Turn Back the Clock*. Since the posters do not as a rule feature the Stooges, however, their value is limited.

Other Stooges movie posters, especially those released between 1934 and 1947, retain considerable value because they feature Curly Howard. Their value may range from $75 to $150, again depending on condition. Of the 190 shorts the Stooges appeared in for Columbia, Curly played the third Stooge in 97. As a rule of thumb, you can expect to pay more for posters promoting the first 100 shorts. (Shemp Howard played through short #174, and Joe Besser finished out the series.)

The most attainable Stooges movie posters promote their starring roles in feature films (*Have Rocket, Will Travel; Snow White and the Three Stooges; The Three Stooges Go Around the World in a Daze*). Be prepared to pay $150–175 for these, depending on the film, condition, and date of release. The Stooges' first starring feature, *Have Rocket, Will Travel*, was released in 1959; their last, *The Outlaws Is Coming*, in 1965.

Where to get them:

Try Jerry Ohlinger's Movie Material Store, Remember When, or Eddie Brandt's Saturday Matinee.

Advertising sheet for posters promoting the feature film *3 of a Kind*, which starred a pre-Stooges Shemp.

LOBBY CARDS

Hand in hand with the movie posters, Stooges lobby cards are popular—and relatively scarce—collectibles. Lobby cards are just that—colorful advertising cards (miniposters, you might say) printed on thick paper or cardboard and displayed in the lobbies of movie theaters showing Stooges films. They're much smaller than movie posters—about 11 by 14 inches—so they can be displayed nicely in a collector's home or office. And just as with the posters, the studios required that the theater return or destroy the card after its initial use. MGM did not release Stooges lobby cards, so the Columbia cards represent the primary issue.

Value

The early cards demand the greatest price—$150–250. Expect to pay slightly more for cards promoting *Woman Haters* (the first Columbia short), *Men in Black* (their only Oscar nomination), and *Fright Night* (Shemp's first short as a regular).

Where to get them:

You're going to have to dig a little to find posters and lobby cards from the Stooges' heyday. Chances are that all the existing items are known, and most of them are in the hands of private collectors. A rule of thumb: if the Stooges are dear to the heart of the guy who owns the item, you're going to pay extra for it. But there are a few alternatives.

Remember When, Eddie Brandt's Saturday Matinee, and Jerry Ohlinger's Movie Material Store have various cards.

Bet you Didn't Know! #1

The Stooges' career with Columbia was challenged even before they made their first starring film. On the day when Moe, the leader of the act, signed with Columbia, Larry was at Universal, signing a different contract for the team. The two studios fought over the rights to the team until someone pointed out that Moe had signed the Columbia deal three hours before Larry inked his pact. Columbia got the Stooges, and that left Universal Studios free to sign another up-and-coming comedy team—Abbott and Costello.

Lobby cards from the Stooges' shorts are almost as fun to look at as the films themselves.

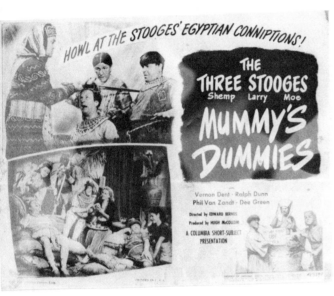

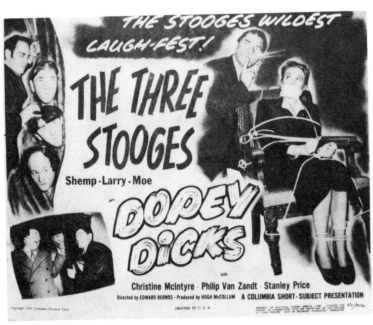

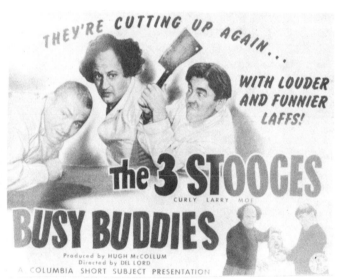

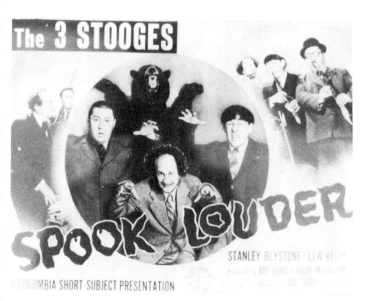

TED HEALY *and his three Southern Gentlemen*

The BIGGEST
LAUGH IN
NEW YORK
•
**A NIGHT
IN
VENICE**
•
Now at the
SHUBERT
THEATRE
Matinees
Wed. and Sat.

This 1920s postcard promoted "Ted Healy and His Three Southern Gentlemen." The boys looked like "southern gentlemen" about as much as Colonel Sanders resembled Shemp.

STOOGE MANIA

ORIGINAL STOOGES POSTCARDS

During the 1920s, the Stooges' likenesses appeared on a handful of postcards promoting their Broadway appearances. These postcards were given out free by the Shubert Brothers, who produced the shows, as promotional pieces. Today, however, these postcards are considered rare, due primarily to their scarcity.

Value

Original Postcards ....$25 each

Where to get them:

Try Eddie Brandt's Saturday Matinee.

Bet you Didn't Know! #2

According to media critic Gary Deeb, young Sam Howard got his nickname—Shemp—from his mother. When she called Sam to dinner, her thick Lithuanian accent produced, "Shem, c'mon home t' dinner." Naturally, it stuck with little Sam's friends, and he became "Shemp" forever.

STILLS

Literally hundreds of Stooge stills, reflecting every aspect of the Stooges' career, are available. If you look hard enough, you can locate original stills; they'll be slightly yellowed and on a much thicker paper than more recent reproductions. Still, when the negative exists, first-quality prints can be obtained. These are among the most popular Stooges collectibles of all. Original Columbia stills can be identified by the stamped information on the back: "Columbia Pictures Corp. Permission is hereby granted to newspaper, magazines, and other periodicals to reproduce this photograph. This picture may not be rented or loaned nor used for advertising purposes." Most of the stills will have a typed cutline glued to the back of the photograph, describing the performers depicted and the title of the film represented. Again, the film and trio portrayed dictate the value of the still.

Value

Originals $25–50
Reprints $3–8

Where to get them:

Most movie memorabilia dealers stock Stooges stills, which have been issued by Columbia Studios for retail purchase. The Classic Movie and Comic Center has a complete line of authorized stills.

If you're looking for original stills, Eddie Brandt's Saturday Matinee stocks all kinds—some you won't find anywhere else.

Serious collectors will want to contact Columbia Pictures directly. The studio still holds copyright privileges on all film-related licensed material and has some rare material in its archives. But it won't come cheap.

In answer to incredible autograph requests, the Stooges sent out ready-made autographed photos such as these. Take a good look at the top photo—that's Shemp's head superimposed on Curly's body!

In this rare non-Columbia still, Larry really seems to be enjoying the lesson in hearing loss.

Chicago's Hotel McCormick advertised celebrity guests during the 1920s, including Ted Healy and his Stooges. That's Fred Sanborn, a part-time Stooge, on the far right.

#3

Curly Howard, a real animal lover, once witnessed the demise of a favorite dog. Curly and his wife, Elaine, were taking a stroll with their pet one afternoon when the dog broke loose and dashed into the street. He was hit by a car and died almost immediately. Curly went berserk with grief but calmed down when brother Moe presented him with a brand-new puppy as a gift shortly afterward.

STOOGE
MANIA

ORIGINAL STOOGES ADVERTISEMENTS

During the late 1920s and early 1930s, the Stooges appeared in a series of advertising cards and newspaper cartoons as a promotional tie-in with various businesses. Often these businesses catered to the vaudeville trade. These promotional items were actual photos of the Stooges accompanied by cartoon-style dialogue. They were frequently run in the entertainment sections of local newspapers.

Value

Original Advertisements..................$5–10

Where to get them:

Try Eddie Brandt's Saturday Matinee.

THE ULTIMATE QUIZ

#1-10

Perhaps the greatest test for any Stooges fan is the possession of intimate—if perhaps meaningless—knowledge. The kind of information only the most faithful, dedicated, and, as a result, bleary-eyed fans can remember. Hence the "Ultimate Quiz," through which you can discover on your own whether you possess "the wrong stuff."

You'll find 100 of the most difficult Stooges questions ever asked interspersed throughout the following pages. Answers are at the end of the book.

1. What are the names of the Stooges' female alter egos in *Self Made Maids* (1950)?

2. What magazine do the Stooges work for in their 1941 short subject *Dutiful but Dumb*?

3. In *Loco Boy Makes Good* (1942), the Stooges appear as nightclub entertainers. How do they bill themselves?

4. *Studio Stoops* (1950) has the boys employed as pest exterminators at a movie studio. What is the name of the studio?

5. The Stooges invade a Hollywood film company presided over by actor Bud Jamison in *Movie Maniacs* (1936). What is Jamison's character's name in this film?

6. What does Shemp accidentally swallow in *Crime on Their Hands* (1948)?

7. In *Malice in the Palace* (1948), the Stooges disguise themselves while attempting to retrieve a stolen gem. What kind of costumes do they wear?

8. The Stooges find themselves in the Army in *Boobs in Arms* (1940). Prior to soldiering, what was their line of work at the opening of the film?

9. What are the Stooges' brides' names in *The Sitter-Downers* (1937), in which the boys are forced to construct their own house?

10. Whom do the Stooges impersonate in *Three Sappy People* (1939) in order to earn some "quick" money?

STILL SHOTS #1

The Stooges have just learned that
A. Moe's tie is actually one of Shemp's argyle socks.
B. Shemp's face has been declared "unfit for public viewing."
C. Larry's graduating class has named him "most likely to resemble somebody's grandma."

Moe Howard sent this photo to fans toward the end of his career, at a time when he was promoting his character-acting abilities.

Bet You Didn't Know! #4

It's common knowledge among Stooges fans that Moe Howard was the business brains of the group, both on-screen and off. But Moe's financial expertise was used for more than just "official" Three Stooges business. He handled much of kid brother Curly's business affairs, advising him on investments and trying to convince him to save his money. Moe even wound up doing Curly's income tax returns for him! But Moe's efforts to convert his partners into businessmen never really paid off. As a retired Larry Fine, then living in a charity rest home, put it, "Moe saved his money—I spent mine." Moe, whom Larry claimed "owned most of North Hollywood," died a millionaire.

A smattering of publicity indicates the Stooges' lasting celebrity.

STOOGES IN THE NEWS

You can add a lot to your Stooges memorabilia collection just by picking up a copy of the daily newspaper. The Stooges have never been more "in the news" than they are right now, even without a full-time public relations department (like they had at Columbia). Most of the ink they're getting today attempts to explain why they're getting ink in the first place. And to that question, there seems to be one answer: popular demand. Syndicated columnist Gary Deeb has been one of the Stooges' most visible supporters; he periodically devotes his entire column to chronicling Stoogemania around the country. "Curly Howard was the most underappreciated comic performer of his time," wrote Deeb. "It's nice to see the Three Stooges get the respect they deserve." Other writers and commentators nationwide also laud the team. In fact, the *Wall Street Journal* recently ran a front-page column on Stoogemania, headlined "The Three Stooges Are Riding a Wave of Adult Adulation."

The first sign of the Stooges' comeback appeared way back in 1959–in *Time* magazine, no less. "The most startling comeback of many a show business season is being staged by a trio of brillo-headed knockabouts called the Three Stooges." The article noted that, once the Stooges' contract ended with Columbia (in January 1958), the studio sold its pre-1948 backlog of films to television. "The trio considered breaking up the act," the article continued, "until TV, that supposed wrecker of old-style comedians, turned out to be their salvation."

Even the critics seemed to be warming up by then, perhaps because the Stooges themselves were slowing down a bit. In a 1961 *New York Times* film review, Howard Thompson wrote the "Stooges, never more subdued, are lively, to be sure. If their friendly, pleasant bumbling (the pies fly only once) doesn't exactly enhance Grimm, the boys do quite nicely as sideline

21

Film 'Stooge' Loses Wife by Divorce

LATimes 6-20-46

Curly Howard, one of the "Three Stooges" of film comedies, yesterday lost Marion, his bride of last October, in a one-day divorce contest before Superior Judge Arthur Crum.

Starting off with 20 charges in her cross-complaint, Mrs. Howard convinced the court that she was the one who was entitled to the decree. A conference between the couple's attorneys netted her $5200 as her share of the community property, and she promised to vacate their North Hollywood home by the middle of next month.

She said he used filthy, vulgar and vile language; kept two vicious dogs which she was afraid would bite her; shouted at waiters in cafes; pushed, struck and pinched her; put cigars in the sink.

He said she refused to live

Curly Howard

with him; she wanted half of everything; called him a bad name at least once.

Howard, whose legal name is Jerome Horowitz, also said that he met his present wife last October in New York, married her two weeks later, but not until after he had given her $250 for clothes, a $3750 mink coat and an $850 wrist watch.

Jerome Howard of Three Stooges Fame Succumbs

Jerome (Curly) Howard, 46, of the famed Three Stooges, vaudeville and film trio, died yesterday at Baldy View Sanitarium of a long illness which followed a stroke in 1946.

He leaves his widow, Mrs. Valerie Howard, and their daughter Janie, 3½; another daughter Marilyn, 11, and two brothers, Moe and Shemp Howard. It was Shemp Howard who succeeded Jerome after illness forced retirement.

Funeral services will be conducted tomorrow at 2 p.m. at Malinow & Simons, 818 Venice Blvd., with interment at Home of Peace Cemetery.

Born in Brooklyn Mr. Howard had lived in California for the past 20 years. The family home is at 11124 Riverside Drive, Toluca Lake.

156 'New 3 Stooges' Cartoons For TV

Heritage International, headed by Skip Steloff, has set coventure with Normandie Productions, headed by Norman Maurer and The Three Stooges, for production of 156 five-minute color cartoons tagged "The New Three Stooges." Total of 29 markets, including the five Metropolitan Broadcasting Co. stations, have been set, latter including KTTV locally and WNEW, New York.

Cartoons, with Maurer exec producer and Dick Brown producer, will begin filming first of next month for airing in the fall. Format is four minutes of cartoons, with one minute of live action featuring the Stooges. Production budget for entire package is $2,500,000, filming to be done locally at Cambria Studios.

Lee Orgell is head writer and production supervisor on animation of the cartoons, with Dave Detiege directing. Syndication deals are for entire package of 156.

Heritage has just completed three features in Europe, among them "City Of Fear," starring Trevor Howard and Terry Moore, which Allied Artists h...

THE WALL STREET JOURNAL.

NO. 56 ★★★   MONDAY, JANUARY 4, 1982

The Three Stooges Are Riding a Wave Of Adult Adulation

* * *

TV, Festivals Show Old Films Of Comic-Abuse Experts; Boon to Columbia Pictures

By FREDERICK C. KLEIN
Staff Reporter of THE WALL STREET JOURNAL

RIVER GROVE, Ill.—It's the weekly meeting of the Triton College film club in this suburb of Chicago, and the assembled scholars have settled in for an evening of film classics. Do they await a picture by Eisenstein, Lang or Hitchcock?

Nope, The Three Stooges.

Stooges Everywhere

Signs of Stoogeomania are numerous. Columbia Pictures, which owns the rights to

all of the 195-odd short films the group made between 1934 and 1958, reports that the movies are being shown by TV stations in 61 "markets" reaching 90% of the U.S. population. Three Stooges film festivals, some of them running for as long as four hours, have been staged recently in theaters in New York, Chicago, Los Angeles and Dallas, among other cities.

"The Stooge Chronicles," a book by Jeffrey Forrester, a 22-year-old Stoogeophile, has sold about 10,000 copies in less than a year. And another book on the group, by Joan Maurer, the daughter of Stooge Moe Howard, is soon to be publ... in Rolling Stone magazin... formation of a Three Stoo... more than 4,000 response... tures, which is using the ... sell a new line of Three S... syndicated comic strip is ...

The financial implica... tivity aren't clear beca... tures, the principal ber... cuss them. The consens... big bucks are involved.

Whi pone show fore a...

T... broa suppl perm pric Poo 198 the ind leac muc...

JEROME "CURLY" HOWARD

Services were held at Malinow & Simon Mortuary yesterday for Jerome "Curley" Howard, 46, one of the original Three Stooges of vaude and pix, who died Friday at Baldy View Sanitorium, San Gabriel, after a lingering illness. Interment was at Home of Peace Cemetery.

With his brother, Moe Howard, and Larry Fine, he made his vaude debut as one of the late Ted Healy's Three Stooges in 1928. Trio formed their own act when Healy died and were featured in a number of Columbia shorts and features. Howard suffered a stroke in 1946 and another brother, Shemp, took his place in the Three Stooges act. In addition to his brothers, he is survived by widow, Valerie, and two daughters.

This 1940s ad promotes a personal appearance by the Stooges. The team made most of its money doing live shows—their films were primarily a means of keeping themselves in the limelight as "movie stars."

Moe—last of Three Stooges, dead at 78

LOS ANGELES (AP) — Moe Howard, the last member of the original Three Stooges comedy team, died Sunday night of lung cancer. He was 78.

Mr. Howard was the slapstick trio's mop-haired leader, whose bullying bluster invariably received its just deserts in the end from his partners.

Mr. Howard was a boyhood friend of comedian Ted Healy and they teamed in a vaudeville act in the early 1920s, which featured Howard heckling Healy from the audience.

Mr. Howard's older brother, Shemp, joined the act in 1925 and the group was expanded shortly after to include Larry Fine, who died late last year.

The group performed under various names but clicked on the vaudeville circuit and on Broadway as Ted Healy and His Stooges.

Signed by MGM, the group featured its unique brand of knockabout comedy in a number of movies, beginning with "Soup to Nuts" in 1930 and "Dancing Lady," which starred Clark Gable and Joan Crawford.

The original group started breaking up, with Shemp leaving to appear solo in MGM comedies. He was replaced by another Howard brother, Jerry, who was called Curly because of his shaven head.

In 1934, Healy left to pursue a career as a character actor and the Three Stooges, as the group renamed itself, left MGM to make a series of short comedy films for Columbia.

They acted under the Columbia banner for the next 24 years. Illness forced Curly's retirement in 1946 and he died in 1952. Shemp died in 1955.

The Three Stooges' membership later included Joe Besser and Joe de Rita.

Moe's obituary acknowledges the end of an era.

An early 1930s clipping reviews an appearance by
Ted Healy and his Stooges.

sponsors of the hero and heroine." Have you
guessed the movie he was referring to? *Snow
White and the Three Stooges.*

Celebrated film historian Leonard Maltin
wrote, in 1972, "just as it was impossible for a
television series to maintain consistently superi-
or quality on a week-to-week basis, so it was
with the prolific Three Stooges. The best of the
Three Stooges shorts can hold their own against
any other shorts made during Hollywood's
golden age of comedy."

SCRIPTS

Perhaps the rarest of all Stooge collectibles, a few original scripts are known to circulate from collector to collector. Pure joy for the ultimate fan, owning an actual Stooge script allows you to engage the services of your family, friends, even small household pets in reliving those golden screen moments. Note: Pets should always be given the part of Curly.

Original scripts are among the most sought-after collectibles.

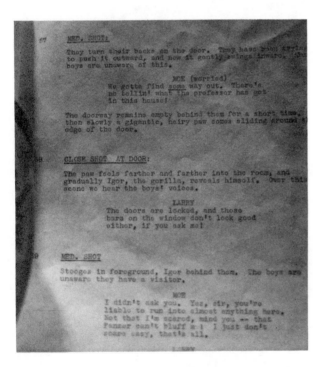

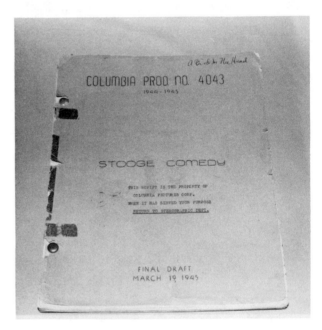

The Stooges short *A Bird in the Head* as it appeared before production. This film was scripter/director Ed Bernds' first Stooges effort.

Value

Original Scripts $350–1,000

Where to get them:

You'll have a hard time locating Stooge scripts, especially since the Stooges' recent surge in popularity. Try Eddie Brandt's Saturday Matinee or Jerry Ohlinger's Movie Memorabilia Store.

STOOGE MANIA

PRESSBOOKS

One of the most amusing collectible items is the movie pressbook, a sheet (or booklet) of ad mats, promotion ideas, and press releases provided by the studio to theaters for promotional consideration. Stooge pressbooks are available only for their feature films of the late 1950s and early 1960s, but they remain a highly sought-after item because of the number of photos included in each book and the sometimes ridiculous promotional ideas offered. For instance, to promote *The Three Stooges Fun-O-Rama*, a festival of Stooge shorts featuring Joe Besser, the pressbook suggests "as an advance giveaway, offer pieces of a promoted fruitcake to patrons with paper napkins imprinted: Nuttier than a Fruitcake! The Three Stooges Fun-O-Rama!"

That'll really pack 'em in.

Pressbook from the feature film *Stop! Look! And Laugh!* (1960), which featured clips from early Stooges shorts.

Value

Stooges Pressbooks .... About $5.

Where to get them:

Most of the movie-oriented dealers, like Eddie Brandt, can help you find them.

Pressbook includes ready-to-submit newspaper columns, photos, and offers for promotional posters.

THE 'STOOGES'

The Three Stooges have always rated among the top comedy teams in motion picture history. Currently, they are leading the pack! Go after a saturation coverage of your community via exploitation stunts, contests and tie-ups and, in addition, get wide distribution of the Three Stooges' stills which are available at National Screen Service (see bottom of page 3).

'NUTTY' NOTES

The Three Stooges have built their well-earned reputation for comedy because of the "nuttiness," and "screwiness" of their screen antics. Use these slang connotations for fun and foolishness as part of your exploitation campaign on "Three Stooges Fun-O-Rama."

- Radio quiz: Deejay to offer guest tickets for first ten phone calls from listeners giving correct names of the comedians: Larry Fine, Moe Howard and Joe Besser.
- Letter write-in: "I Like the Three Stooges Because . . ." for best 10-word description of a "stooge," or of the Three Stooges.
- Post school bulletin boards; offer guest tickets for the Three Stooges.
- Prizes for TV imitators of the Three Stooges.
- Present guest tickets to teen-agers who have the best laughs, demonstrated on a radio or TV show, or in the theatre lobby.
- Set up ballot box in advance in lobby and suggest youngsters vote for their favorite Three Stooges comedy.
- Wherever possible, go after local sponsors using Three Stooges comedies on TV, for tie-ups, contests, stunts covering your engagement of the "Three Stooges Fun-O-Rama!"

DRIVE-IN'S

- One spectacular stunt that should get your patronage in the mood for "Three Stooges Fun-O-Rama," one that may be worked anywhere but should be very effective for a drive-in theatre, is a pie-throwing contest. Youngsters volunteering should come prepared, dressed in bathing suits! Entries are judged on their accuracy and girls as well as boys can compete. Contestants should bring along their regular clothes to be donned after the wash-off with hoses.
- Imprint your "Three Stooges Fun-O-Rama" playdate on every napkin, paper tray, etc., possible. Make sure the kids see it too, in the playground area!
- Giveaway envelopes containing three peanuts, imprinted with copy: "Do You Like Nuts? See 'Three Stooges Fun-O-Rama' State Theatre! Now Playing!"
- Place a number of nuts in a glass bowl and offer guest tickets to those guessing closest to the correct number: "Nuttier Than Nuts in a Bowl! 'Three Stooges Fun-O-Rama!' Coming! State Theatre."
- As advance giveaway, offer pieces of a promoted fruitcake to patrons with paper napkins imprinted: "Nuttier Than a Fruitcake! 'Three Stooges Fun-O-Rama!' State Theatre."
- Enclose teaser copy with all nuts sold at theatre, neighborhood stores, etc. "The 'Nuts Are Coming! Watch for Next Week's Show at the State Theatre!"
- Tie baggage tags to large screws, imprint with copy: "You May Not Have a Screw Loose But You Should See 'Three Stooges Fun-O-Rama!' It's the Screwiest!"
- Spread a large quantity of screws in a window of a cooperating store presenting guest tickets for those submitting nearest guesses to correct number.

Style B   Style A

TWO TELOPS

Style A is a 10-second spot with identification shared by the TV station. Style B is intended to carry theatre and playdate imprint only. Price of each telop: $7.50 with imprint; $5.00 without imprint; $2.00 for each additional slide or telop of the style ordered. When you order, be sure to specify the style of the telop and the imprint copy you want. Order well in advance of playdate direct from: QQ Title Card Co., 247 West 46th St., New York 36, N.Y.

LAUGH 'EM UP!

Play up the hilariousness of the "Three Stooges Fun-O-Rama" by advertising a reward, in a newspaper and on a lobby 40" x 60", for any teen-ager who can watch the picture and not even smile! Those who volunteer should be seated in a group in the center of the theatre, watched by a judge. A laughing crowd sound effects record, for p.a. play, record No. 5002B, is available direct from: Thomas J. Valentino, Inc., 150 West 46th Street, New York 36, N.Y.

RADIO SPOT

15 SECONDS: You'll laugh! You'll howl! You'll rock! You'll yowl! It's the "Three Stooges Fun-O-Rama!" Special feature-length laugh treat! Columbia Pictures' "Three Stooges Fun-O-Rama!" State Theatre! Now playing!

THE 'THREE'

The actual number "3" can be used to promote "Three Stooges Fun-O-Rama." Use these ideas to promote the number at the same time crediting the title:

- Deejay contest offering listeners guest ticket prizes for other famed comic groups like "The Three Stooges," such as the Marx Brothers, etc.
- Prizes for the most expressions using the number three, such as "two is company, three's a crowd," "three on a match," etc.
- Guest admit first ten sets of three brothers coming to the boxoffice, or triplets.

STOOGES STILLS

A set of five stills from Three Stooges comedies is available at National Screen Service. This set is composed of the following: Still No. 1902-3 (from "Guns A' Poppin'"), Still No. 1904-4 (from "Rusty Romeos"), Still No. 1911-8 (from "Oil's Well That Ends Well"), Still No. 4251-4 (from "Hoofs and Goofs") and Still No. 4253-5 (from "Space Ship Sappy").

Pressbook from *The Three Stooges Fun-O-Rama* includes such nutty suggestions to theater owners as spreading hundreds of screws under a sign stating, "You may not have a screw loose but you should see 'The Three Stooges Fun-O-Rama'! It's the screwiest!"

Hey Winch!
Take to the hills!
Take to the shelters!
The ORIGINAL THREE STOOGES
are loose! They're running wild in a rib-cracking uproarious RIOT OF SLAPSTICK!
Monkeys is the craziest people!
Mr. Stubbs of Toby Tyler fame!
Columbia makes the funniest pictures!
I'M LARRY!
I'M CURLY!
I'M MOE!
'STOP! LOOK! AND LAUGH!'
co-starring
Paul WINCHELL
with JERRY MAHONEY and KNUCKLEHEAD SMIFF
and featuring
THE MARQUIS CHIMPS
OFFICER JOE BOLTON
Cinderella sequence directed by LOU BRANDT
Produced and written by SID KULLER
Paul Winchell sequences directed by DON APPELL
Associate Producer MARTHA VERA ROMM
Produced by HARRY ROMM · Directed by JULES WHITE
A HARRY ROMM Production · A COLUMBIA PICTURES Release

26

STOOGEMANIA

(Mat 2-A; Still No. 22) The Original Three Stooges, Larry, Moe and Curly, are at their zany best in the Harry Romm production for Columbia Pictures, "Stop! Look! And Laugh!" Also starred are ventriloquist Paul Winchell and his dummies, Jerry Mahoney and Knucklehead Smiff. The Marquis Chimps and Officer Joe Bolton are featured in the uproarious comedy.

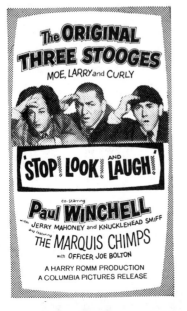

Accessories

- 1 SHEET
- 3 SHEET
- 8 11 x 14's
- 22 x 28 (SLIDE the same)
- INSERT CARD
- TRAILER

• 3 Sheet   • 1 Sheet

- 40 x 60, 30 x 40, 24 x 82 DISPLAYS
- THREE STILLS SETS (25 horizontals, 10 uprights, pressbook set)   • COMPOSITE MAT

VIDEO STOOGES

You can now see the Stooges on more than 50 television stations in major cities throughout the country. And you don't have to wait until midnight, either. Stooges shorts consistently score high ratings in time slots traditionally reserved for more conservative programming. There are Stooge specials, too, devoted entirely to various aspects of the team's career.

The first of these specials to hit the airwaves was *The Stooge Follies*, a two-hour celebration of the Stooges' film career featuring classic clips, Stooges music videos, and special insights by movie critic Gene Siskel and media critic Gary Deeb. And, believe it or not, when the program premiered in Chicago, it racked up a higher rating than that of all three networks combined.

There's also a film documentary, *Fifty Years with the Stooges*, that covers the Stooges' career from their vaudeville years to the DeRita days. Narrated by Steve Allen, this hour-long program features interviews with Stooge director Ed Bernds, producer Jules White, actor Emil Sitka, and various Stooges' relatives.

And—it had to happen—Columbia Pictures recently announced its intention to produce several new "Stooges" theatrical films, the first of which would be titled 003 *Stooges*. Former Stooges producer Norman Maurer is in charge. A national talent search for three stooges is planned.

And what could be better than all your favorite Stooges shorts in one midnight showing at the local theater? Showing the movies in your own home, of course. Now you can get your fix anytime, day or night, with any one of several videotape collections of shorts now available. But you have to be careful in making your selections—some of the shorts appear in more than one collection.

The Three Stooges Volume I
  A Bird in the Head (1946)
  Dizzy Pilots (1943)
  Three Sappy People (1939)

The Three Stooges Volume II
  Uncivil Warriors (1935)
  Three Missing Links (1938)
  Micro-Phonies (1945)

The Three Stooges Volume III
  Pop Goes the Easel (1935)
  Calling All Curs (1939)
  An Ache in Every Stake (1941)

The Three Stooges Volume IV
  Woman Haters (1934)
  Three Little Beers (1935)
  Tassels in the Air (1938)

Value: $39.95

Where to get it:

Columbia Pictures Home Entertainment.

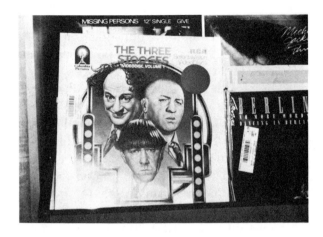

Popular Stooges shorts are also available on videodisc.

The Three Stooges Festival
Disorder in the Court (1936)
Sing a Song of Six Pants (1947)
Malice in the Palace (1949)

Where to get it:

Discount Video Tapes. The contents of this tape are available under various other titles. Ask your local video dealer.

Value: $39.95

WHY YOUR MOTHER WOULDN'T LET YOU WATCH THE STOOGES

If you grew up watching the Stooges on television, you're familiar with at least a dozen reasons why the Stooges were no good for you. Never mind that you no longer hear militant parents, outraged by the force with which Moe "influenced" his charges, rallying to ban the shorts from the airwaves. You probably still remember how valiantly you fought for the right to watch them.

Argument #1: "You get too excited. You'll try to part your brother's hair with the hacksaw again."

Argument #2: "You get too excited. You'll try to reorganize the plumbing again."

Argument #3: "You get too excited. You'll put your sister's eye out."

Argument #4: "You get too excited. You'll try to iron the cat again."

Argument #5: "You get too excited."

Nametags bearing the names and likenesses of the Stooges were issued at the "Stooge Follies" party. Guests were forced to wear them throughout the evening.

Invitation sent to members of the local media inviting them to the premiere screening of "The Stooge Follies." The party featured roving Stooge impersonators, a custard pie-throwing contest, and a giant video-screen presentation of "Stooge Follies" highlights. Guests included such famed Stooge supporters as syndicated columnist Gary Deeb, movie historian Greg Lenburg, and a host of local television and radio personalities.

WFLD TV PRESENTS

The Stooge Follies

SUNDAY, FEBRUARY 26TH
NOON TIL 2PM

When you think of classic slapstick comedy, who *can* you think of but the Three Stooges? Who can honestly say they've never mimicked the hilarious antics of America's beloved Moe, Larry and Curly? Well, get ready for the best of the Three Stooges on WFLD TV/Channel 32's "The Stooge Follies."

See clips from over 100 of the classic Three Stooges movies, including segments you may have never seen before! You'll see the *complete,* full-length version of classics like "All the World's a Stooge," "Dizzy Doctors," "Hoi Polloi," and "Sweet Pie and Pie." *And,* you'll have a chance to join the boys for the greatest pie-fight ever filmed.

"The Stooge Follies," a WFLD TV presentation, is written and narrated by Jeffrey Forrester ("The Stooge Chronicles," "Stoogephile Trivia Book"), and produced by Forrester and WFLD TV's Jon Findley.

32 WFLD TV
METROMEDIA

Press release for the television special "The Stooge Follies."

Bet you Didn't Know! #5

When the Stooges signed with Columbia in 1934, each member—Moe, Larry, and Curly—made about $20,000 per year. Twenty-four years later, after some 200 films, their salaries had ballooned to . . . $20,000. They never received a raise.

Gold Raiders, the only feature-length film that included Shemp as one of the Three Stooges, was released in England as an 8mm home movie. Note that Curly, not Shemp, is illustrated on the box top.

Imagine three dimensions of Stooges right in your own home! This Super-8 release attempted to capitalize on the 3-D craze. It didn't.

STOOGE MANIA

STOOGES ON FILM

Traditionalists can still purchase film versions of the Stooge shorts, though, with age, they're becoming harder to find. The most popular format for Stooge films was, until recently, Super 8. The emergence of videotape has all but eliminated the market for these films, which in turn is making them collectors' items of sorts. You can expect to pay $8–10 for a recent edition—you can still find them in some discount/variety stores—but their value is slowly rising.

The diehard fan, the aficionado, the ultimate viewer, if you will, collects the Stooges' shorts on 16mm. This sort of habit is expensive, especially with the availability of videotape versions of many of the shorts. However, unless you're dilligent enough to tape the shorts from local television broadcasts (and you don't tape commercial interruptions), 16mm remains the only way to go if you want to collect them all.

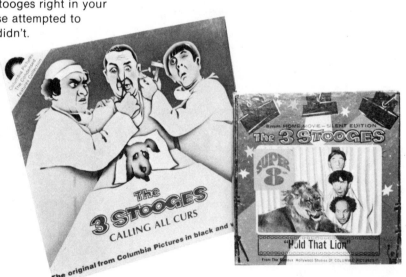

Two popular—and with the advent of videotape, relatively scarce—8mm Stooges releases: *Hold That Lion* and *Calling All Curs.*

Why is Shemp smiling? Because he just got top billing in this title frame from a Stooges short.

STARRING SHORT SUBJECTS

Available on 16 MM:

- A Bird in the Head
- A-Ducking They Did Go
- A Gem of a Jam
- A Merry Mix Up
- A Missed Fortune
- A Pain in the Pullman
- A Plumbing We Will Go
- A Snitch in Time
- All Gummed Up
- All the World's a Stooge
- An Ache in Every Stake
- Ants in the Pantry
- Baby Sitters' Jitters
- Back from the Front
- Back to the Woods
- Bedlam in Paradise
- Beer Barrel Polecats
- Blunder Boys
- Boobs in Arms
- Booby Dupes
- Booty and the Beast
- Brideless Groom
- Bubble Trouble
- Busy Buddies
- Cactus Makes Perfect
- Calling All Curs
- Cash and Carry
- Commotion on the Ocean
- Cookoo Cavaliers

- Corny Casanovas
- Crash Goes the Hash
- Creeps
- Crime on Their Hands
- Cuckoo on a Choo Choo
- Disorder in the Court
- Dizzy Detectives
- Dizzy Doctors
- Dizzy Pilots
- Don't Throw That Knife
- Dopey Dicks
- Dunked in the Deep
- Dutiful but Dumb
- Even as I.O.U.
- False Alarms
- Fiddlers Three
- Fifi Blows Her Top
- Flagpole Jitters
- Flat Foot Stooges
- Fling in the Ring
- Flying Saucer Daffy
- For Crimin' Out Loud
- Fright Night
- From Nurse to Worse
- Fuelin' Around
- Gents in a Jam
- Gents without Cents
- G.I. Wanna Go Home
- Goof on the Roof
- Goofs and Saddles
- Grips, Grunts and Groans

- Guns a Poppin'!
- Gypped in the Penthouse
- Half-Shot Shooters
- Half Wits Holiday
- He Cooked His Goose
- Healthy, Wealthy and Dumb
- Heavenly Daze
- Higher than a Kite
- Hoi Polloi
- Hokus Pokus
- Hold That Lion
- Hoofs and Goofs
- Horses Collars
- Horsing Around
- Hot Ice
- Hot Scots
- Hot Stuff
- How High Is Up?
- Hugs and Mugs
- Hula-La-La
- Husbands Beware
- I Can Hardly Wait
- Idiots Deluxe
- Idle Roomers
- If a Body Meets a Body
- I'll Never Heil Again
- I'm a Monkey's Uncle
- In the Sweet Pie and Pie
- Income Tax Sappy
- Knutzy Knights
- Listen, Judge

16 mm Shorts Continued

- ☐ Loco Boy Makes Good
- ☐ Loose Loot
- ☐ Love at First Bite
- ☐ Malice in the Palace
- ☐ Matri-Phony
- ☐ Men in Black
- ☐ Merry Mavericks
- ☐ Micro-Phonies
- ☐ Monkey Businessmen
- ☐ Movie Maniacs
- ☐ Mummy's Dummies
- ☐ Muscle Up a Little Closer
- ☐ Musty Musketeers
- ☐ Mutts to You
- ☐ No Census, No Feeling
- ☐ No Dough, Boys
- ☐ Nutty but Nice
- ☐ Of Cash and Hash
- ☐ Oil's Well That Ends Well
- ☐ Oily to Bed, Oily to Rise
- ☐ Out West
- ☐ Outer Space Jitters
- ☐ Pals and Gals
- ☐ Pardon My Backfire
- ☐ Pardon My Clutch
- ☐ Pardon My Scotch
- ☐ Pest Man Wins
- ☐ Phony Express
- ☐ Pies and Guys
- ☐ Playing the Ponies
- ☐ Pop Goes the Easel
- ☐ Punch Drunks
- ☐ Punchy Cowpunchers
- ☐ Quiz Whiz
- ☐ Restless Knights
- ☐ Rhythm and Weep
- ☐ Rip, Sew and Stitch
- ☐ Rockin' through the Rockies
- ☐ Rumpus in the Harem
- ☐ Rusty Romeos
- ☐ Sappy Bull Fighters
- ☐ Saved by the Belle
- ☐ Scheming Schemers
- ☐ Scotched in Scotland
- ☐ Scrambled Brains
- ☐ Self Made Maids
- ☐ Shivering Sherlocks
- ☐ Shot in the Frontier
- ☐ Sing a Song of Six Pants
- ☐ Slap Happy Sleuths
- ☐ Slippery Silks
- ☐ So Long, Mr. Chumps
- ☐ Sock-A-Bye Baby
- ☐ Some More of Samoa
- ☐ Space Ship Sappy
- ☐ Spook Louder

- ☐ Spooks
- ☐ Squareheads of the Round Table
- ☐ Stone Age Romeos
- ☐ Studio Stoops
- ☐ Sweet and Hot
- ☐ Tassels in the Air
- ☐ Termites of 1938
- ☐ The Ghost Talks
- ☐ The Sitter-Downers
- ☐ The Three Troubledoers
- ☐ The Tooth Will Out
- ☐ The Yoke's on Me
- ☐ They Stooge to Conga
- ☐ Three Arabian Nuts
- ☐ Three Dark Horses
- ☐ Three Dumb Clucks
- ☐ Three Hams on Rye
- ☐ Three Little Beers
- ☐ Three Little Pigskins
- ☐ Three Little Pirates
- ☐ Three Little Sew and Sews

- ☐ Three Little Twirps
- ☐ Three Loan Wolves
- ☐ Three Missing Links
- ☐ Three Pests in a Mess
- ☐ Three Sappy People
- ☐ Three Smart Saps
- ☐ Tricky Dicks
- ☐ Triple Crossed
- ☐ Uncivil Warbirds
- ☐ Uncivil Warriors
- ☐ Up in Daisy's Penthouse
- ☐ Vagabond Loafers
- ☐ Violent Is the Word for Curly
- ☐ We Want Our Mummy
- ☐ Wee Wee Monsieur
- ☐ Wham-Bam-Slam!
- ☐ What's the Matador?
- ☐ Who Done It?
- ☐ Whoops I'm an Indian
- ☐ Woman Haters
- ☐ Yes We Have No Bonanza
- ☐ You Nazty Spy!

STARRING FEATURE FILMS AVAILABLE ON 16MM:

- ☐ Have Rocket, Will Travel
- ☐ The Outlaws Is Coming
- ☐ The Three Stooges Go Around the World in a Daze
- ☐ The Three Stooges in Orbit
- ☐ The Three Stooges Meet Hercules

Value:

Price will vary depending where you find the films; expect to pay between $75–200.

Where to get them:

Contact the 3 Stooges Fan Club for availability.

Moe Howard was known throughout show business as a man of great generosity. He would often spearhead charity drives for various organizations and loved to buy groceries for the less well-to-do. Comedian Emil Sitka once accompanied Moe on a food-gathering outing, along with two of Sitka's young sons. During the course of the grocery shopping, Moe invited the two boys to fill up a cart of their own with luxury food for themselves. "You know," said Moe, "things you usually don't get at home." Moe was more than a little surprised when the Sitka boys returned with a cart full of everything from caviar to chocolate-covered ants! But Moe wasn't about to humiliate the boys by forcing them to return the expensive items—Moe put the stuff back himself.

STOOGE MANIA

STOOGES ON TELEVISION

Although the Stooges have television to thank for their current—and greatest—popularity, for a long time it looked like television wasn't right for the team. They had struggled to sell a number of pilots during the 1960s; before that, they were bound by an agreement with Columbia that prohibited them from appearing regularly on television. They made guest appearances, though, on many popular programs, including "Texaco Star Theater" and the "Ed Sullivan Show." The sponsors viewed the Stooges as children's entertainment, but the Stooges' violent brand of humor was viewed as a drawback on television. Interestingly enough, their largest audience nowadays isn't made up of children at all, but of adults—many of them the children of the 1960s.

This rare television magazine cover marks the Stooges' resurgence of popularity in the early 1960s.

One Stooges series stands out, though, because it achieved success—it made it to the screen. "The New Three Stooges" aired in the mid-1960s and is still shown in some markets. The program combined live-action segments with animated Stooges cartoons.

ANIMATION CELLS

An interesting collectible arose out of all this—the animation cell, original artwork produced on celluloid sheets that were used to film the cartoon portions of the series.

Value

Animation cell...........................$75–125

Artwork from a completed but never aired pilot, produced in the identical format, also turns up occasionally. The work is, however, inferior and commands a slightly lower price. The pilot? "The Three Stooges Scrapbook."

Value

From $50–100, depending on the characters depicted and the amount of artwork which appears.

Where to get them:

Contact Stooge collectors through the fan clubs.

"TV Jitters" features rarely seen television footage of the Stooges.

Recently, a videotape capturing the essence of the Stooges on television has surfaced—TV Jitters. The 90-minute cassette features footage of the Stooges from their television appearances in the early 1950s, clowning with such stars as Frank Sinatra, Louis Armstrong, Ed Wynn, and others. Much of the footage has not been seen on television in more than 30 years.

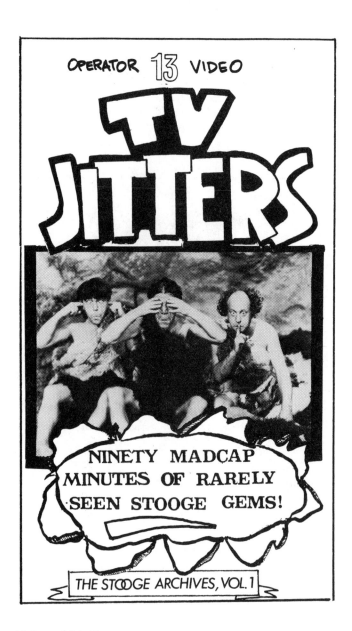

Value: $39.95

Where to get it:

Operator Thirteen Video.

STOOGE MANIA

ONE OUTSTANDING REASON TO READ A BOOK: "KOOK'S TOUR"

Norman Maurer's "Kook's Tour," the ill-fated comedic travelogue that has yet to air on television.

A 1970 Stooges television pilot, "Kook's Tour," was originally planned to follow the escapades of the Stooges as they traveled around the world. The Stooges, however, were too tired to travel (Moe was 71, and Larry was right behind), and they didn't want to endure the physical beating their traditional comedy required. So, in September 1969, they compromised and filmed the pilot in Idaho. Moe and Larry refused even to wear their trademark haircuts. Sadly, Larry suffered a debilitating stroke after only three-fourths of the pilot had been filmed, forcing producer Norman Maurer to fill in the remaining portion with scenery. "Kook's Tour" was rejected through television channels but found its way to distribution through Niles Films as a Super-8 feature, in color with sound, for $200. Niles Films declared bankruptcy in 1981. Periodically rumors surface of the pending release of "Kook's Tour" to television, but as yet the travelogue has not been aired even on local television.

Moe Howard and Joe DeRita confer on the set of one of the team's pilot film efforts in the 1960s.

Kook's Tour, the Stooges' "last and funniest film," as the package proclaims, in Super-8.

Value

"Kook's Tour" Pilot (Super-8) $200

Where to get it:

Some collectors may have copies. Contact the Stooge fan clubs.

STOOGES FILM FESTIVALS

One of the more recent phenomena of Stoogemania is the Three Stooges Film Festival. Events featuring the best of the team's Columbia shorts have sprung up all over the country, with wildly successful results.

In Chicago, for example, Three Stooges Festivals are on a par with movie premieres and sneak previews. A special Stooges festival held at the Granada Theater in 1983 drew more than 1,000 people. Described by festival management as "well behaved but extremely vocal" in its appreciation of the Stooges, the crowd went wild with excitement when the first Stooges film was projected. Festival manager Bill Rosman explains: "In *Ants in the Pantry*, there is a scene where mice fall down the back of an elderly gentleman, and he dances wildly to get rid of them. The Stooges, naturally, join in. The audience began clapping their hands and joining in, too. And when the Stooges did their famous 'Swingin' the Alphabet' number, the audience sang along. And they didn't miss a word!"

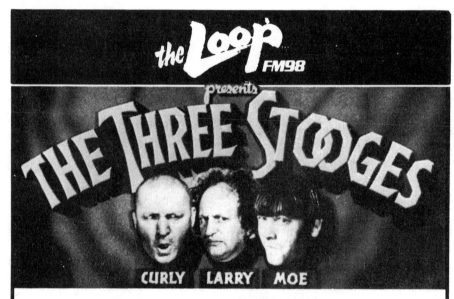

Recently in Pittsburgh, however, a riot broke out at a local screening of Stooges shorts. The reason? The theater's management had mistakenly booked a Shemp episode instead of a Curly episode. The reaction was violent, as Curly supporters reportedly began trashing the theater!

A similar reaction occurred in response to a screening of MGM's *Three Stooges Festival*, which is actually a collection of shorts the team made while working with Ted Healy in the early 1930s. Many fans, anticipating their favorite episodes from Columbia Pictures, were horrified to discover that shorts such as *The Big Idea* and *Plane Nuts* give the Stooges very little to do in comparison with Healy. The novelty of the MGM collection is that the films have yet to be released to television and, for the most part, haven't been seen theatrically in some 50 years. In addition, some of the films in this package were shot in a primitive Technicolor process.

By far, it's the Columbia Curly shorts that bring down houses whenever they're shown.

The Stooges, like many stage and screen performers, observed various superstitions throughout their careers. Moe avoided whistling whenever he was in a dressing room. And in the early vaudeville days, and later when he toured the country with Larry Fine and Joe DeRita, Moe refused to send out his laundry for cleaning until *after* the first performance was over. He was afraid it might jinx the show. And Moe would always avoid lighting three cigarettes on one match.

Larry's favorite superstition? "Never throw your hat on a bed."

Poster of this charmer is available through the Three Stooges Club, Inc.

STOOGE MANIA

MORE POSTERS

In order to satisfy the insatiable Stooges fan's appetite, on-the-ball merchandisers are turning out Stooges memorabilia even as you read this.

The Stooge still poster is perhaps the most popular item being produced today. Walk into any college dormitory, and you'll see more Stooges posters than textbooks. One of the ways you can get a Stooges poster is to join the Official Three Stooges Fan Club, run by Norman Maurer Productions.

Value

Still Posters ....About $5

Where to get them:

One source for posters is the Classic Movie and Comic Center.

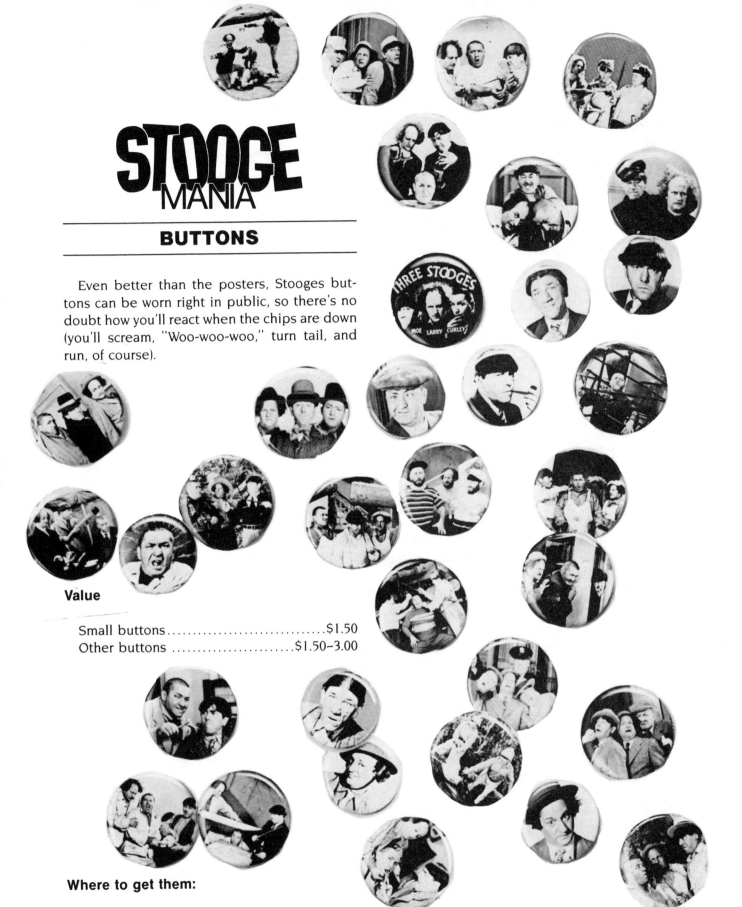

STOOGE MANIA

BUTTONS

Even better than the posters, Stooges buttons can be worn right in public, so there's no doubt how you'll react when the chips are down (you'll scream, "Woo-woo-woo," turn tail, and run, of course).

Value

Small buttons.............................$1.50
Other buttons $1.50–3.00

Where to get them:

Los Angeles Button Company, Button Up Company, or Classic Movie and Comic Center. Try your local record store, too.

The ultimate badges of honor, as worn by Stooges fans everywhere.

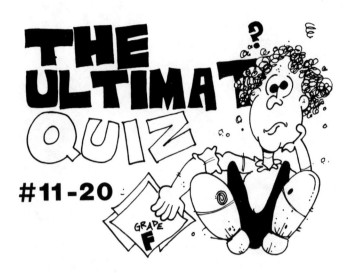

THE ULTIMAT QUIZ #11-20

11. What is the name of the graveyard in which the Stooges plan to bury a mannequin in *Three Pests in a Mess* (1945)?

12. What is the name of the Stooges' boss in *Horses' Collars* (1935), which has the boys as detectives sent out West?

13. Who threw the pies in the Stooges' 1943 short subject *Spook Louder*?

14. What is the name of the crook played by Benny Rubin in the Stooges' "Dragnet" spoof, *Blunder Boys* (1955)?

15. What is the character name of Shemp's homely bride in *Scrambled Brains* (1951)?

16. Who plays the role of the Stooges' pal, Bill, in their 1953 short subject *Goof on the Roof*?

17. What is the name of the Stooges' hotel in *Healthy, Wealthy, and Dumb* (1938)?

18. In *If a Body Meets a Body* (1945), Curly's character name is Curly Q. Link. What does the Q stand for?

19. Shemp finds a magic lamp in *Three Arabian Nuts* (1950). What is the first thing he wishes for?

20. Curly and Larry drive Moe to the brink of hysteria with their noisy musical rehearsing in *Idiots Deluxe* (1945). What is the name of their musical act?

Bet you Didn't Know! #8

The Stooges have attained everlasting popularity since their films were released to television in 1959. But they have never made a cent on residuals or royalties, due to a clause in their contract. "When we made our deal in 1934," Moe recalled, "there was no TV, and the studio had a clause in our contract that gave Columbia the rights to our voices, our likeness, and so on—into perpetuity. That means forever."

In 1960, the Stooges addressed the Screen Actors Guild in an attempt to gain TV royalties for pre-1960 movies. They were rejected.

The president of the Screen Actors Guild at the time? Ronald Reagan.

STOOGE MANIA

THE PILLSBURY PROJECTOR

One of the rarest Stooges articles is a projector that was produced as a promotional giveaway for theaters showing Stooges films. The projector is not much more than thick cardboard, folded into the shape of a movie viewer, with a hand-crank that, when turned, flipped individual frames depicting the Stooges. When you got it going, the frames (actual film reproductions printed on cardboard squares) gave the illusion of movement. Because this item, which was produced in 1935, is rare, it is highly sought by collectors.

There is also a poster advertising the projector and explaining the promotion to filmgoers. And at the time of issue, store displays and other advertising materials were also released, but few of those items exist today.

Lobby stand-up used as part of the Pillsbury "Moving Picture Machine" promotion.

Value

Projector $100–150
Poster $50

Where to get them:

Ask Gasoline Alley Antiques.

The Stooges show off promotional photos produced as a tie-in for the Pillsbury/Farina "Moving Picture Machine."

STILL SHOTS #2

These guys are to music what
  A. Itzchak Perlman is to slapstick farce.
  B. Larry "Bud" Melman is to male modeling.
  C. Margaret Thatcher is to slam dancing.

CLUBBING THE STOOGES

The very reason the Stooges legend exists today is fan adulation. No comedy team—or movie team, for that matter—has ever had a more faithful (and rabid) following than the Stooges. Naturally, these fans have banded together from time to time in celebration.

The Three Stooges Club, Inc., offers a membership card and the *3 Stooges Journal*, plus Larry Fine's real-life brother (Moe Feinberg) as president, to member fans. That's Moe on the cover of the newsletter.

There are two Stooges fan clubs operating today, and both claim to be official. To complicate matters further, both clubs have a familial link to the Stooges. The Three Stooges Club, Inc., is run by Moe Feinberg, Larry Fine's brother. The Official Three Stooges Fan Club is operated by Norman Maurer, son-in-law of Moe Howard. Both clubs offer merchandise for sale and keep members up to date on Stooges events.

The Official Three Stooges Fan Club features a membership card, certificate, newsletter, and poster offers as an incentive to join the ranks.

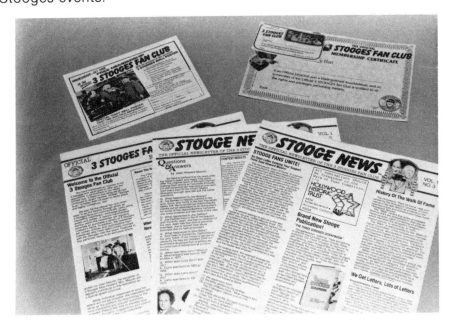

The Three Stooges Club, Inc., was sanctioned in 1974 by the Three Stooges—Moe Howard, Larry Fine, and Joe DeRita—as the official club for Stooges fans, but that hasn't calmed the controversy. It offers a six-times-a-year newsletter plus membership card for $6. You can contact the club at 1207 Hellerman St., Philadelphia, PA 19111.

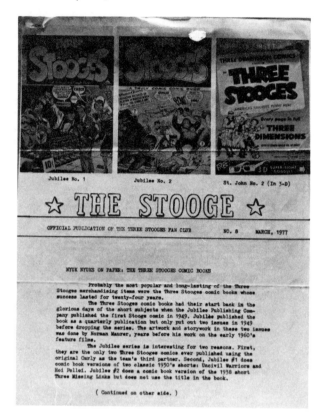

Sometimes even fans get into the collectibles act. This mid-1970s newsletter (issued to members of the Three Stooges Fan Club) is often sought for anecdotes and photographs of memorabilia. It was issued before the first Stooges books were written.

The Official Three Stooges Fan Club will send you a membership certificate, card, newsletter, and poster for $5. Write to PO Box 266, Mt. Morris, IL 61054.

Stooges fans aren't limited to the United States, either. The Three Stooges Appreciation Society is a group of Australian fans who have met regularly for more than a decade to "celebrate our mutual interest."

SLAM-BAM—THANK YOU, CURLY

Did you ever wonder who was the first modern dancer to incorporate floor burns into the act? Or who, while unceremoniously attached from behind by a spring, single-handedly created slam dancing? No, not Fred Astaire. Not Gene Kelly. It was Curly Howard, the original breakdancer, creator of the now classic shoulder spin. Think about *that.*

TOUR THE USA STOOGES-STYLE: A
MINI-VACATION FOR DEDICATED FANS ONLY

You can take your own kook's tour by following this handy guide to great Stooges sites across America. So pack up your bags and hit the road for the oddest odyssey you're ever likely to encounter.

Begin in Brooklyn, New York, the birthplace of Stooges Moe, Shemp, and Curly. Then we'll hit the road for Philadelphia, Pennsylvania—the birthplace of Larry Fine. While we're there, we'll look for the theaters in which Larry began his career: the Allegheny, Broadway, Keystone, and Nixon's Grand.

Then it's off to St. Louis (birthplace of Joe Besser), to Stooges, a nightclub that features glasses with likenesses of the Stooges printed right on them. We'll watch the Stooges on late-night television, which has in recent years become a St. Louis tradition. Fans throw "Stoogie Bashes" every Friday and Saturday night when the Stooge shorts are broadcast on local TV after midnight.

Head north to Hammond, Indiana, and stop for lunch at the Three Stooges Deli. This place boasts of such delicacies as "Larry's Log" (ham, salami, and provolone cheese), "Curly's Combo" (ham, turkey, and Swiss cheese), and "Moe's Muffalotta"—you decide what's in that one. The owner is a member of the Three Stooges Club, so you'll feel comfortable here.

Then it's on to Chicago for a visit to the Three Stooges Oldies Bar, which features a huge wall mural of Curly, Larry, and Moe flanking the bar's owners. While you're in town, why not drop by the Rainbow Gardens? That's where Moe and Shemp first met Larry Fine in 1925.

Now it's time to move on west toward Lincoln, Nebraska, home of the Stooges Club. This place features a two-story Stooges portrait adorning one wall. Inside, we'll meet Nebraskan Stooges fans—many sporting Stooges Club T-shirts—and we'll get a free drink when we display our Stooges token (which we popped $2 for in the first place).

Had enough? No? Then head out to Hollywood, California, and check out the Stooges'

Even in Wall Street garb, the Stooges look ready to slap at a moment's notice.

shining star on Vine Street, just around the corner from Hollywood Boulevard. The star is across the street from the Merv Griffin Theater and, we might add, across the street from Stooges producer Jules White's star. The Stooges' star is flanked on one side by the star for Chester Conklin, the Keystone comedian who appeared in many of the Stooges' funniest shorts. And while you're in town, don't forget to drop by the old Columbia Pictures complex on Gower Street. Columbia no longer occupies these buildings, but these are the very same soundstages where Stooge history was made in the 1930s, '40s, and '50s.

Bet you Didn't Know! #9

The Stooges devoted time—and money—to various charities over the years and spent many off days visiting children in hospitals. Their favorite charity was the Spastic Children's Guild—they subsidized a wing of the Guild's Hillside House in Santa Barbara, California. At one point, the Stooges were donating nearly $30,000 a year to the guild home, with help from such notables as Danny Thomas, Jerry Lewis, and Red Skelton.

A STAR SHINES ON THE STOOGES

As most movie fans know, film stars are commemorated on the Walk of Fame in Hollywood. Major stars, like Slim Whitman, Harry Von Zell, and Rin Tin Tin, are represented. But for years, the Stooges were denied a place on the walk. Toward the end of his life, Moe made several attempts to obtain for the Stooges their well-deserved place but was flatly refused by the Hollywood Chamber of Commerce—unless he forked over $1,500 (the original stars—1,500 of them—were issued free). Was it the "lowbrow" violence inherent in their films that was keeping the Stooges out? Or was it that their career was spent producing only short subjects—the "filler" before the feature? Moe died before he could find out the answer. "It's just a shame that my dad couldn't have seen it happen, because he did feel bad about it," Moe's daughter Joan recalls.

Joe Besser and Stooge well-wishers gleam as the star is unveiled.

Moe did, however, make one last-ditch effort to fulfill his dream when, in 1975—shortly after Larry Fine had died and only four months before he would, too—Moe told Chicago radio personality Eddie Schwartz, "They can keep their star, and I'll tell them where to put it—one point at a time." Schwartz began a bid to gain national attention for the Stooges' slight and even ventured to Hollywood to lobby in person. Eventually syndicated radio personality Gary Owens—along with Stooge historians Jeff and Greg Lenburg—launched the national campaign that eventually won the Stooges their star. In time, more than 20,000 letters were received by the Hollywood Chamber of Commerce, and the cost of the star ceremony—which had risen to $3,000—was donated anonymously.

Uncle Miltie's salute to the Stooges is interrupted by Joe Besser's effeminate hijinks.

Favorite Stooges supporting actor Emil Sitka was one of the most popular celebrities attending the star ceremony.

On August 30, 1983—more than five decades after the Stooges began their career—the Three Stooges were recognized with a star on the Walk of Fame in Hollywood. More than 2,500 fans were in attendance, including Stooges relatives, associates, and a few famous friends, like Milton Berle, who paid a lasting tribute to the team. "Their longevity is because what they do is timeless," Berle said. "They don't do anything verbal. Everything is physical. All this shtick will be around long after the zoo has closed in San Diego—after every comic, or condition. It's endless." He concluded his speech by saying, "The boys are in heaven, entertaining my mother."

Oh, yes—the event boasted the largest attendance for a star ceremony in Hollywood history. Would Moe have enjoyed that last laugh!

The star—commemorating 50 years of Stooging—as it appears today.

CHARACTERISTIC QUOTES #1-6

Can you identify which Stooge said what line, simply by the tone of the sentence?

1. "I'm sorry, Moe, it was an accident!"

2. "I'll knock your head right through your socks!"

3. "I'll tear that cucumber of yours off and shove it down your throat!"

4. "Are you casting asparagus on my cookin'?"

5. "Oh, took me illiterately, eh?"

6. "Wait a minute! There must be some mistake!"

Answers are in the Appendix.

21. In *Saved by the Belle* (1939), the Stooges are clothing salesmen plying their trade in the Latin American country of Valeska. What is the name of the ruler in power there?

22. The Stooges try to break a man out of prison in *So Long, Mr. Chumps* (1941). What is his name?

23. What is the name of the union the Stooges belong to in both *Half-Wits Holiday* (1947) and *Pies and Guys* (1958)?

24. Why does Vernon Dent refuse to buy a duck-hunting club membership in *A-Ducking They Did Go* (1939)?

25. Who plays the role of theater critic Nick Barker in the Stooges' 1950 short subject *Three Hams on Rye*?

26. What are the Stooges' names in *Matri-Phony* (1942), which has them as potters in ancient times?

27. *Slap Happy Sleuths* (1950) has the Stooges employed as detectives for a large oil company. What is the name of the company?

28. In *Some More of Samoa* (1941), the Stooges play tree surgeons who are sent to a tropical island on assignment. What's the name of the island?

29. Who plays the role of Shemp's long-dead uncle in both *Heavenly Daze* (1948) and *Bedlam in Paradise* (1955)?

30. What medicine are the Stooges peddling in *Dizzy Doctors* (1937)?

STOOGESEARCH

Can you find the titles of 19 Stooges films hidden in this puzzle? (Titles can be formed horizontally, vertically, diagonally, and backward.)

```
P  U  N  C  H  D  R  U  N  K  S  L  I  C
Q  S  L  I  P  P  E  R  Y  S  I  L  K  S
U  T  S  P  A  L  S  A  N  D  G  A  L  S
I  A  P  P  H  O  T  I  C  E  A  B  O  O
Z  H  O  I  P  O  L  L  O  R  R  L  G  U
W  H  O  D  O  N  E  I  T  P  E  S  T  T
H  O  K  H  O  T  S  T  U  F  F  E  T  W
I  T  S  H  O  T  S  C  O  T  S  S  P  E
Z  B  N  G  H  O  K  U  S  P  O  K  U  S
G  E  N  T  S  I  N  A  J  A  M  R  H  T
R  B  O  O  B  S  I  N  A  R  M  S  Y  V
H  O  I  F  R  I  G  H  T  N  I  G  H  T
M  A  T  R  I  P  H  O  N  Y  L  O  R  I
P  K  O  O  K  S  T  O  U  R  S  B  O  L
S  E  E  R  H  T  S  R  E  L  D  D  I  F
```

Answers are in the Appendix.

STOOGE MANIA

T-SHIRTS

What more could fans want than to wear the Stooges' colors—black and blue, of course—wherever they go? If nothing else, Stooges shirts give fans a place to pin their buttons.

They come in all shapes and sizes, some with photographs, others with artwork. But you have to be careful when wearing a Stooge T-shirt. They mark you as an easy target for pie-lobbing weirdos lurking about all across America.

Value

T-shirts ....Between $5–15

Where to get them:

The Three Stooges Club markets several types, ranging in price from $5.50 to $7.50. The Classic Movie and Comic Center is another resource. And Artwear features several unique designs produced especially for them.

Truly devoted fans show their loyalty by wearing any one of the many T-shirts on the market today.

Shemp Howard was once named "The Ugliest Man in Hollywood"—by his own agent! He concocted the scheme as a means of getting Shemp's name into the limelight. Surprisingly, there seemed to be no other contestants willing to enter the contest.

STOOGES WIGS

No, you don't have to undergo the humiliation of shaving your dome just so you can look like Curly when you render your famous imitation at parties and funerals. Now you can purchase Frizz, Bowl, and Crew-cut wigs to wear instead. There are even latex masks of your favorite Stooges, if you really want to go off the edge.

Value

Contact the manufacturer for prices.

Where to get them:

Nat Cooper manufactures a variety of latex products to help you live a life of lunacy. Visit your local costume shop or variety store.

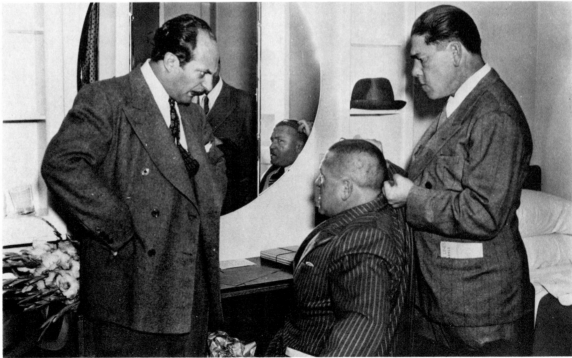

Larry and Moe attempt to rearrange Curly's scalp in this publicity still.

PUPPETS

Beautifully crafted hand puppets were produced in 1935, each an accurate reproduction of one of the Stooges' mugs. They are now considered scarce, and those you can find command a high price.

A second version of Stooges hand puppets was sold in the 1960s, manufactured by the Jefferson Manufacturing Company. They can easily be differentiated from the earlier puppets by comparing the expressions on the faces as well as noting the hand-covering cloth; the 1960s puppets wear printed clothing, while the earlier ones are plain.

There are finger puppets, too, which were mass-produced in the early 1960s, as well as a ventriloquist dummy version of Moe, to help you vent your frustration vicariously.

Value

Hand Puppets (1935)...................$75–100
Hand Puppets (1960s)...................$50–75
Finger Puppets $5–10
Ventriloquist Dummy.......................$25

Where to get them:

Gasoline Alley Antiques specializes in toy-related merchandise and usually has a few Stooges puppets on hand.

Stooges fan Donald Jacka poses with a few of his most prized collectibles, including a "Moe" ventriloquist dummy.

STOOGES RECORDS

The Stooges' recording career can best be described as peculiar. The records—originally numbering 15, but new and bootlegged versions appear almost every day—feature simple children's songs and stories, as the bulk of their recorded material was produced during the peak years of the Stooges' television popularity. Two records stand out among the rest— *Snow White and the Three Stooges* and *The Three Stooges Nonsense Songbook*. The *Snow White* album is actually a soundtrack recording of the film by the same title and is popular among collectors for the dialogue, lifted directly from the soundtrack. In fact, the album contains the song "Looking for People, Looking for Fun," which was ultimately trimmed from the film.

The Three Stooges Nonsense Song Book features a few Big Band standards and contains "The Alphabet Song," an adaptation of the "Swingin' the Alphabet" song from the 1938 classic Stooge short *Violent Is the Word for Curly*.

Not every record contains unique material, either, so you have to watch what you buy. Two singles, "The Princess and Pea" and "The Lamp," were first issued on the *Three Stooges in Storyland* album. And *The Three Stooges Sing For Kids* is actually *The Three Stooges Nonsense Song Book* minus two songs, "Two Little Birdies" and "Peggy O'Neil." Don't ask why.

Lately, small record companies have reissued several Stooges records under new titles. There's even a picture disc to give you something to look at while you listen.

The Three Stooges and Six Funny Bone Stories, a 1973 rerelease of *The Three Stooges in Storyland* album.

Value (Albums)

The Three Stooges—Madcap Musical Nonsense at
   Your House $5
Snow White and the Three Stooges................$25
The Three Stooges Nonsense Songbook............$10
The Three Stooges Sing for Kids...................$8
The Three Stooges in Storyland $5
The Three Stooges and Six Funny Bone Stories....$4
Yogi Bear and the Three Stooges Meet Dr. No-No $7

The Stooges on 45 RPM—and as the subject of popular records today.

In one of the strangest marketing decisions ever, the Stooges recorded 238 different versions of "The Three Stooges Happy Birthday Record"— each with a different child's name. Merchants had difficulty stocking all 238 versions in any appreciable quantity, so Erics everywhere had to settle for a Joshua or a Norman version. The venture failed shortly after the records were released.

Value (45s)

"Have Rocket, Will Travel" $3
"The Three Stooges Sing" $3
"The Three Stooges Come to Your House" ..$3
"Sinking of the Robert E. Lee" $3
"The Three Stooges Happy Birthday
   Record" $1.50
"The Three Stooges Meet the Princess and the
   Pea" $3
"The Three Stooges and the Magic Lamp" ..$3

Value (EP—extended play)

The Three Stooges Sing Six Happy Yuletide Songs $4

Where to get them:

Contact collectors through the fan clubs.

CURLY'S SHUFFLE

Although the Stooges turned out more than a dozen albums over the course of their career, they never came close to cracking the Top 40. Or the Top 140, for that matter. Then how did they wind up with the number 1 song in Chicago and in *Billboard's* national Top 15 in 1984?

Peter Quinn can answer that question. He's the author and composer of "The Curly Shuffle," and his Jump 'n the Saddle band surprised itself with the hottest record in the country in early 1984. It was after a live performance, band member T.C. Furlong recalls, and Quinn was dancing backstage. "Somebody asked what Peter was doing. Quinn said, 'You know, what Curly does. The Curly Shuffle.' " Various Curlyisms had been part of Quinn's act for years, including the now-famous two-step. Quinn went home that night and, inspired, knocked off the lyrics to the song within an hour. When the band later included the song in one of its live shows, the audience went wild.

The Jump 'n the Saddle band scored a national hit with "The Curly Shuffle."

But it took a Stooges fan club member to get big-time exposure for the song. At the urging of a local Stooges—and Jump 'n the Saddle—fan, the band wrote to Stooges fan club president Moe Feinberg to see if the club was interested in buying and distributing the "Curly Shuffle" record. Feinberg expressed interest, but the band hesitated after asking how many records the club could sell. "He said their last record sold only 75 copies," Furlong recalls, "so we got the thing going on our own."

It didn't take long for Chicago disc jockeys to discover the song, and after WGN radio's Roy Leonard debuted the record on his show, requests for the song came pouring in. Soon stations all over the country were playing the song—and stations of every format, at that. "I think the only stations that didn't play it were the Moody Bible Institute and the beautiful music stations," Furlong exclaims. With the national demand, the band soon landed a recording contract with industry giant Atlantic Records, and as of this writing, the song has sold some one million copies.

"I'm a fan—not a fanatic," Quinn says. "But I like them a lot. I get real pleasure watching grown men drag each other around by the nostrils. And I've been watching them ever since my mother said I couldn't."

Value

$2 or $3 for the single, about $10 for the album. Check your local record store.

Where to get them:

"The Curly Shuffle" is available through Atlantic Records. The song is also featured on Jump 'n the Saddle's *Jump 'n the Saddle Band* album, also distributed by Atlantic. Check your local record store.

THE CURLY SHUFFLE

When me and my friends go out on the town
We can't sit still, we can't sit down
We don't like to fight and we don't like to scuffle
But we dance all night doin' The Curly Shuffle.

Hey Moe, hey Moe
Well uh nyuk nyuk nyuk
La dee dee La dee dee
Woob woob woob woob woob woob woob woob woob
Well we never miss a chance
We get up and dance and do The Curly Shuffle.

Well me and my friends love Larry and Moe
We love Curly's brother Shemp and his fat clone Joe
It's such a delight to boogie and hustle
Dancin' all night to The Curly Shuffle.

Hey Moe, hey Moe
Well uh nyuk nyuk nyuk nyuk
Wee bee bee bee bee bee bee bee
Oh wise guy
Well we never miss a chance
We get up and dance and do The Curly Shuffle.

Well me and my friends we all love to see
Comedy Classics on late-night TV
Those knuckleheads love to get in a scuffle
They push and they shove doin' The Curly Shuffle.

Hey Moe, hey Moe
Well uh nyuk nyuk nyuk nyuk
Look at the grouse, look at the grouse
Ruff-ruff
Well we never miss a chance
We get up and dance and do The Curly Shuffle.

We do The Curly Shuffle (what'd ya say?)
We do The Curly Shuffle (that's what I thought ya said!)
We do The Curly Shuffle (nyuh-uh)
We do The Curly Shuffle (soitenly!)
Well we never miss a chance
We get up and dance and do The Curly Shuffle.

The original ACME version of "The Curly Shuffle," now a collector's item.

DO THE CURLY SHUFFLE

Curly really started something when he threw his first fit. Now Stooges the world over are following in his footsteps. Follow this handy guide and shuffle the Curly way!

· THE SHUFFLE.

1. As the music rolls ("The Curly Shuffle," of course), place your right leg in a bent position directly behind your back. Lean your body forward and, with a flip of your arms, simultaneously slide your left foot backward while planting your right toes into the ground. Got it? Repeat this sequence again and again until it's second nature to you. You're shufflin'!

2. With your body facing front and center, perch yourself on one leg and twist—violently, recklessly—from side to side, arms flailing to and fro. Perform this maneuver whenever a slight rest period is in order.

3. As your legs pound furiously into the dance floor, beat yourself about the head and shoulders; Curly's favorite form of self-flagellation is not only fun to watch; it helps clear the sinuses, too.

4. By this time, you should be halfway across the dance floor, with little chance of reuniting with your partner. To get back to where you began, perform the simplest maneuver of all—head back, arms free, legs nimble, gut thrust forward (kind of a poor man's broad jump)—and let your momentum carry you back to where you began (or the approximate vicinity, anyway).

Repeat these four steps over and over—you're doing The Curly Shuffle. Hey Moe! Hey Moe!

A 1961 article discusses the Stooges' comeback on television, including a surprising popularity in Australia.

The Stooges were little guys. Moe and Larry checked in at only 5 feet 4 inches, and Shemp and Curly stood 5 feet 5 inches. Big Joe Besser towered at almost 5 feet 6 inches. And Joe DeRita stood only 5 feet 3½ inches tall.

This late 1950s article was prompted by the release of "75 of the Three Stooges Movie Shorts for TV." Thus began the Stooges' second wave of popularity.

THE ULTIMATE QUIZ #31-40

GRADE F

31. What are the Stooges' character names in *Goofs and Saddles* (1937), in which they portray undercover agents?

32. In *Cuckoo on a Choo Choo* (1952), the Stooges wreak havoc aboard a derailed passenger train car. What's the name of the railroad that owns the car?

33. What is Larry's occupation in both *He Cooked His Goose* (1952) and its remake, *Triple Crossed* (1959)?

34. The Stooges are searching for the mummy of King Rutentuten in *We Want Our Mummy* (1939). During the search, they stumble across the mummy of his wife. What is her name?

35. In *Rhythm and Weep* (1946), a "wealthy producer" (Jack Norton) turns out to be an escaped lunatic. What is the name of the asylum he escaped from?

36. Shemp plays a music professor who must get married in *Brideless Groom* (1947) or forfeit a $500,000 legacy. As the story begins, how much time does he have left to find a wife?

37. The Stooges play war veterans awaiting the arrival of their sweethearts in *Love at First Bite* (1950). Where did each Stooge meet his respective fiancee?

38. Moe plays a tyrannical dictator, Hailstone, in *You Nazty Spy* (1940). What is Hailstone's occupation at the opening of the film?

39. Who plays the role of the Stooges' dying father in *Restless Knights* (1935)?

40. What is the character name of the hypnotist featured in both *Hokus Pokus* (1949) and its reworking, *Flagpole Jitters* (1956)?

Moe gets some bad news in this scene from *Brideless Groom* (1947).
That's Stooges stalwart Emil Sitka on the right.

STILL SHOTS #3

Who is this man really?
A. James Coco, with more hair and less weight.
B. Imogene Coca, with more weight and less hair.
C. Bozo choking on a chicken bone.

THE THREE STOOGES FUN HOUSE GAME

Released in 1959, this game was intended for children but probably bored even the simplest mind within a few hours. From the directions: "Just imagine the side-splitting fun of playing in a real amusement park fun house. Picture the hi-jinks as you and your friends actually slide your playing pieces down the giant stand-up Slide or on top of the Barrel of Fun or try to go through the Whale's mouth without it snapping closed. So hold onto your funnybone!"

We're holding, we're holding.

Value

The Three Stooges Fun House Game......$3

Where to get it:

You can probably still find this game in attics and garages today, but if you can't, try Gasoline Alley Antiques.

PUZZLES

One of the ways a Stooges fan spends idle time (that portion of the day when the Stooges aren't airing) is building puzzles—of the Stooges, of course. There are many to choose from. Curly puzzles are the most popular.

Value ....About $5

Where to get them:

Many retail department stores carry Stooge

The Stooges' answer to Monopoly was this "Fun House Game," released by the Lowell Toy Company.

puzzles. If you can't find them, contact other collectors through the fan clubs.

Colorforms issued a Stooges jigsaw puzzle in 1959.

Value

Colorforms Jigsaw Puzzle: $3

Where to get them:

Check Gasoline Alley Antiques.

CHARACTERISTIC QUOTES #7-12

Again, identify the Stooge by the line of dialogue given. Can you name the film as well?

7. "Well, I couldn't help it!"

8. "It's real! A real chimney-panzee!"

9. "Maybe he's in solitary refinement!"

10. "I'll tear your esophagus out and shove it right in your eye!"

11. "You shut up or I'll push that eye right through the back of your head!"

12. "Wait a minute, now, I was only foolin'!"

Answers are in the Appendix.

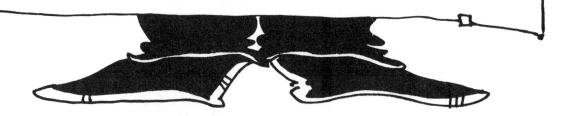

Moe and Curly "steppin' out" in a 1930s photo.

CROSSWITS WITH THE STOOGES

Test your knowledge, lamebrain. See how many Stoogeisms you can identify.

ACROSS

1. Insult hurled by Moe; pertains to fist
7. Nickname indicating lack of brain power
8. Acknowledged leader of the pack
9. Initials of fifth film Stooge
10. Favored Stooge descriptor; refers to tree
12. What Curly is to the village
13. Shortened version describes Larry well
15. How Moe got their attention
16. Weighty description of all six Stooges
17. Initials of fattest Stooge
19. Would-be pet name for Larry
23. Sewing scholar
24. _____Totsy, the Mummy Queen
29. Fiddler's stage name
33. Moe's version of hearing aid; applied to ears

DOWN

2. Dull dome
3. Any large adversary
4. Partly smart
5. Larry's intellectual outlook
6. Shemp's double Palma
11. Mental magpie
13. Initials of oldest Stooge
14. _____ *In a Jam*
18. Curly's cap
20. Initials of Moe's oldest brother
21. _____ *Dough, Boys*
22. Popular movie character Larry resembled
25. Big Cheese Healy
26. Jerome's moniker
27. She blew her top
28. Now-famous nickname originally meant "henchman"
30. It was in the pantry
31. Your average Stooge waistline condition
32. *Three Arabian_____s*

NYUK NYUK!

Curly

Larry

Moe

The three most popular Stooge trading cards—Moe, Larry, and Curly. The back of Curly's card states that he "retired several years ago"—in actuality, Curly Howard had been dead for seven years when these cards were released.

STOOGE MANIA

BUBBLE GUM CARDS

The Stooges are featured on two different sets of trading cards, and one is much more attractive than the other (although both were produced by the same company—Fleer).

"Three Stooges" is a 96-card set, produced in 1959. The cards are in full color and picture the Stooges in various situations, with wacky dialogue printed below. The backs feature short copy about the Stooges' career. Following is a complete card-by-card checklist.

☐ (1)   Curly
☐ (2)   Moe
☐ (3)   Larry
☐ (4)   You'll Sleep in the Room . . .
☐ (5)   They Went Thatta-Way!
☐ (6)   Hey Moe, Don't You Think . . .
☐ (7)   Uh! Uh! I've got . . .
☐ (8)   I Told You Wise Guys . . .
☐ (9)   You Lied! . . .
☐ (10) Come on, Give Back . . .
☐ (11) There's 4 Needles . . .
☐ (12) Hold Still . . .
☐ (13) C'mon Curly . . .
☐ (14) I Tell You . . .
☐ (15) Don't Worry . . .
☐ (16) You Can't Keep Your Money . . .
☐ (17) See No Evil . . .
☐ (18) One More Rehearsal . . .
☐ (19) Hey Fellows . . .
☐ (20) How Do You Like This . . .
☐ (21) Peek-a-BOO!
☐ (22) What Do You Think . . .
☐ (23) Not Even George Washington . . .
☐ (24) Look Out Below.
☐ (25) Next Time . . .
☐ (26) The "Tree" Stooges.
☐ (27) Somehow I have . . .
☐ (28) What Happened . . .
☐ (29) Your Nose Is Too Big . . .
☐ (30) This One's in the Bag.
☐ (31) Bargain Hunters
☐ (32) Cleaning Up . . .

Dinner music.

Popular Stooge trading cards feature the Stooges at their nutty best. The set is difficult to find in "mint" condition.

Value

"Three Stooges" (1959) ....$125 (set)
....$1 (card)
......................................$15 (wrapper)

Let me know when my number comes up.

Now you know where we got all that corn!

Larry plays by ear!

- ☐ (33) Let Me Know . . .
- ☐ (34) Birds of a Feather.
- ☐ (35) Who's That Goodlooking . . .
- ☐ (36) Get Your Nose . . .
- ☐ (37) I Told You . . .
- ☐ (38) Contact!
- ☐ (39) If You Don't Stop . . .
- ☐ (40) I Never Miss . . .
- ☐ (41) About Face!
- ☐ (42) A Hair Raising Experience.
- ☐ (43) No Down Payment.
- ☐ (44) No Use . . .
- ☐ (45) Dig That Crazy . . .
- ☐ (46) Singing in the Shower.
- ☐ (47) Just Thought . . .
- ☐ (48) Larry Plays . . .
- ☐ (49) Always on the Go.
- ☐ (50) Rome Wasn't Burned . . .
- ☐ (51) Be Careful . . .
- ☐ (52) It Must Have Been . . .
- ☐ (53) That's an Order . . .
- ☐ (54) I Could Have Sworn . . .
- ☐ (55) When You Hear . . .
- ☐ (56) Just a Little . . .
- ☐ (57) That Oughtta Hold . . .
- ☐ (58) Curly Always Did . . .
- ☐ (59) Did You Have to . . .
- ☐ (60) Betcha 8 to 5 . . .
- ☐ (61) We Never Took . . .
- ☐ (62) Congratulations Curly . . .
- ☐ (63) Curly, the First Thing . . .
- ☐ (64) Checklist . . .
- ☐ (65) Dinner Music.
- ☐ (66) He Has 40 Teeth . . .
- ☐ (67) Curly, I Tell You . . .
- ☐ (68) Quick—Call . . .
- ☐ (69) What Are You Planting . . .
- ☐ (70) C'mon You Guys . . .
- ☐ (71) Getting Even . . .
- ☐ (72) Give Me Back . . .
- ☐ (73) Bang!
- ☐ (74) Just Don't Break Anything!
- ☐ (75) Take Me to . . .
- ☐ (76) Now You Know . . .
- ☐ (77) Where Has That . . .
- ☐ (78) Good Health Means . . .
- ☐ (79) I Hate to Say This . . .
- ☐ (80) You Say It Was . . .
- ☐ (81) He Must Be Around . . .
- ☐ (82) This Looks Like a Bad . . .
- ☐ (83) Is There a Doctor . . .
- ☐ (84) Strong Backs . . .
- ☐ (85) Give Me a Hand . . .
- ☐ (86) Round and Round . . .
- ☐ (87) Nobody Leave . . .
- ☐ (88) At Least . . .
- ☐ (89) Why Are Fire Engines . . .
- ☐ (90) What's Wrong . . .
- ☐ (91) That's Using Your Head . . .
- ☐ (92) He's Got a Good . . .
- ☐ (93) We Didn't Do Anything . . .
- ☐ (94) I Tell You Your Nose . . .
- ☐ (95) Sorry, This Line Is Busy!
- ☐ (96) Trying the Squeeze Play.

Colorful Fleer trading cards are a highly sought collectible. Complete sets are hard to come by. More on pages 74–75.

Your nose is too big and your brain is too small.

Is there a d

"Three Stooges" is also the title of a 66-card set released in 1965 to promote the film *The Outlaws Is Coming!* The cards are printed in black and white, and dialogue appears beneath each photo. The backs combine to form a huge poster from *The Outlaws Is Coming* film. Following is a complete checklist.

☐ (1) Mac: How's This . . .
☐ (2) Joe: Do You Know . . .
☐ (3) Larry: You Got It . . .
☐ (4) Simple Way . . .
☐ (5) Moe: No Wonder . . .
☐ (6) Joe: I Realize . . .
☐ (7) Larry: Lay off . . .
☐ (8) "My Latest . . .
☐ (9) Joe: This Ain't . . .
☐ (10) Moe: These Martians . . .
☐ (11) Moe: If You Think . . .
☐ (12) Joe: The Instrument . . .
☐ (13) Larry: I'll Hafta . . .
☐ (14) Joe: Underneath . . .
☐ (15) Wearing Bunny Suits . . .
☐ (16) Moe: Do It Yourself . . .
☐ (17) Moe: Singing's Just . . .
☐ (18) Moe: It's Supposed . . .
☐ (19) Moe: But, Landlady . . .
☐ (20) Joe: We Would Have Made . . .
☐ (21) Joe: So We Get Life . . .
☐ (22) Moe: To Heck with . . .
☐ (23) Moe: Just Our Casual . . .
☐ (24) Joe: We Better Blow . . .
☐ (25) Moe: They Said We'd Make . . .
☐ (26) Initiation Night . . .
☐ (27) Joe: It's a Wrist Watch . . .
☐ (28) Larry: So We're Gonna . . .
☐ (29) Moe: Talk about Luck . . .
☐ (30) Moe: Grand Vizier . . .
☐ (31) Moe: If This Doesn't . . .
☐ (32) Moe: Thought I Might . . .
☐ (33) Larry: These Chinese . . .

☐ (34) Larry: They Say Paintin' . . .
☐ (35) Joe: We'd Like a Patent . . .
☐ (36) Moe: The Way Joe . . .
☐ (37) Moe: A "Pal" Shipped Him . . .
☐ (38) Joe: Pioneerin' Suits Me . . .
☐ (39) Joe: Mebbe We Oughta . . .
☐ (40) Moe: Thanks, Ma'am . . .
☐ (41) Moe: Calm Down! . . .
☐ (42) Moe: Since We've Been . . .
☐ (43) Moe: Take That Back . . .
☐ (44) Joe: We'll Be Safe . . .
☐ (45) Larry: These Horse Pistols . . .
☐ (46) Moe: It's More Comfortable . . .
☐ (47) Moe: There's Gonna Be a Law . . .
☐ (48) Joe: Larry, Here, Was . . .
☐ (49) You Can Lead a Stooge . . .
☐ (50) Joe: We Want a Raise . . .
☐ (51) Joe: You Only Get . . .
☐ (52) Joe: You're Gettin' Closer . . .
☐ (53) Joe: You're Just the Type . . .
☐ (54) Bartender: Drink Up . . .
☐ (55) Joe: I Thought These . . .
☐ (56) Joe: Moe, I Wish I Knew . . .
☐ (57) Moe: Begin Operation . . .
☐ (58) Joe: The Redskins Are . . .
☐ (59) Joe: Him Called Chief . . .
☐ (60) Moe: We're New Sioux.
☐ (61) Moe: I Was Lookin' . . .
☐ (62) Joe: Dinner Wouldn't . . .
☐ (63) Moe: Think I'll Spring . . .
☐ (64) Joe: When the Human Bulldozer . . .
☐ (65) Joe: I Know My Own . . .
☐ (66) Moe: Only One Reason . . .

A hair raising experience.

Moe: Give me a buttered muffin.

Larry: One muttered buffin, coming up.

Curly: You mean a buffered muttin?

Larry: No, he wants a muffered buttin.

Moe: Aw forget it. Make it a doughnut.

SEE THE THREE STOOGES in the Columbia Feature Film, "HAVE ROCKET, WILL TRAVEL"

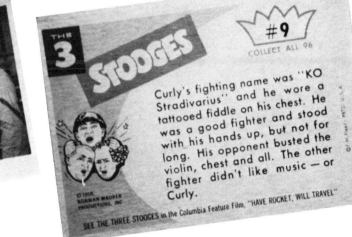

Curly's fighting name was "KO Stradivarius" and he wore a tattooed fiddle on his chest. He was a good fighter and stood with his hands up, but not for long. His opponent busted the violin, chest and all. The other fighter didn't like music — or Curly.

SEE THE THREE STOOGES in the Columbia Feature Film, "HAVE ROCKET, WILL TRAVEL"

The backs of Stooges trading cards contained gags that were reminiscent of the shorts. Not surprising—they were written by Stooges scripter Elwood Ullman.

The busy schedule that the Three Stooges must keep means they also must stay in top physical condition. Larry, Moe, and Curly do this by getting plenty of sleep and eating three good meals a day. They hope all their fans will do the same.

SEE THE THREE STOOGES in the Columbia Feature Film, "HAVE ROCKET, WILL TRAVEL"

Value

"Three Stooges" (1965) ....$60 (set)
....$.75 (card)
....$5 (wrapper)

Where to get them:

Try Eddie Brandt's Saturday Matinee or The Card Coach Company.

Larry: Either his head's too hard or this knife's too dull.

Moe: O.K., forget it. I'll get the lawn mower.

SEE THE THREE STOOGES in the Columbia Feature Film, "HAVE ROCKET, WILL TRAVEL"

The five major Stooges books, all released within the past dozen years. *Stroke of Luck* (front row, left) is extremely scarce and is reportedly no longer in print.

#13

Shemp Howard was a close friend and neighbor of Billy Gilbert, the character comedian who appeared as the crazy patient in the Stooges' *Men in Black*. Shemp and Gilbert even went into the chicken business together, raising their own poultry and splitting the costs between them. But when one of the birds was found dead, Gilbert sadly reported to Shemp that "one of *your* chickens died." Shemp decided to get out of the chicken business shortly thereafter.

BOOKING THE STOOGES

Until a few years ago, you couldn't find anything written on the Stooges, with the exception of an occasional piece by Leonard Maltin. Now there are several major books about the team, covering virtually every historical aspect.

Stroke of Luck (1973) by James Carone is actually Larry Fine's memoirs, published after his retirement from Stooging. Many photos from Larry's own collection are included. Due to extremely limited distribution, this book is considered scarce. (Siena Publishing)

Value: _____$35

Where to get it:

Contact the 3 Stooges fan club.

Moe Howard and the Three Stooges (1977) is, as the title suggests, Moe's version of how the Stooges came together and how they achieved success in more than five decades of Stooging. Loaded with terrific photos from Moe's personal collection. (Citadel Press)

Value: **$8.95**

The Three Stooges Scrapbook (1982), by Joan Howard Maurer and Jeff and Greg Lenburg, is an ambitious look at the Stooges from the fan's point of view, with plenty of photos. Includes historical documentation as well as remembrances by Maurer—Moe's daughter—and husband/producer/manager Norman Maurer. Features an introduction by former Stooge Joe Besser. (Citadel Press)

Value: **$18.95**

The Stooge Chronicles (1981), by Jeffrey Forrester, is a history of the Stooges as remembered by associates, friends, and relatives. Many rare photos from family album collections. (Contemporary Books)

Value: **$7.95**

The Stoogephile Trivia Book (1982), by Jeffrey Forrester, is just that—hundreds of bits of trivial information to challenge the Stooges fan's memory. Includes a foreword by Gary Deeb and a preface by John Candy. (Contemporary Books)

Value: **$6.95**

Where to get them:

Check your local bookstore or comic book store.

Stoogeism Anthology (1977), edited by Paul Fericano, is a light, nostalgic look at the Stooges' career through poems and stills. It should be noted that this book was among the first to commemorate the Stooges at the start of their rebirth of popularity. (Scarecrow Books)

Value: **$3.95**

Where to get it:

Contact the 3 Stooges fan club.

And, reportedly, Joan Howard Maurer is preparing a new book featuring excerpts from classic Stooges movie scripts. The book is scheduled for publication by Citadel Press.

THE STOOGES HOROSCOPES—YOUR SECRETS REVEALED

Now, for the first time, you can learn about yourself just by looking to the stars—provided the stars happen to be named Moe, Larry, Curly, Shemp, Joe, and Curly Joe. Which Stooge do you like best? Never mind which was the most talented, well-versed, best-looking—er, forget that one—just decide which one really gets you down deep. Are you a Curly? A Shemp? Or, heaven forbid, you're not a Moe, are you?

IF YOU ARE A MOE . . .

You're cranky. Maybe miserable, even. You like to take charge, and that's why your credit's so lousy. You derive pleasure from beating your friends and relatives—one reason why only your third-cousin Bernice showed up at your last dinner party, and *she* was carrying a garbage-can lid. You're stuck in a dead-end job, but you're determined to fight your way to the top. After all, you're management material—as long as you have two other idiots to step on.

IF YOU ARE A CURLY . . .

You're the life of the party—for the first five minutes. Then, as you continue to bark at each woman who comes through the door (RUFF! RUFF!), the host leads you by the ear into the alley. You're ebullient, joyous, and about 35 pounds overweight. You were the first one on your block to wear high-water pants—and not be aware of it.

Popular Stooges supporting player Emil Sitka as he appeared in *Merry Mavericks*, a Shemp short from the early 1950s.

IF YOU ARE A SHEMP . . .

You're the funniest member of your family—or so you keep reminding them. Pets occasionally relieve themselves on your trousers. There's more oil on your scalp than in the Persian Gulf. You're perpetually number 2, but it's not as if you're not trying. You once memorized the entire dialogue from *Goof on the Roof*, but you forgot who said what. You sleep naked only because you can't locate your pajamas.

IF YOU ARE A LARRY . . .

Your posture needs improvement. So does your haircut. You're inert. Your father once mistook your shining dome for an ashtray and emptied his pipe in your ear. You've never dated but were once close enough to a woman to see into her blouse. You didn't recognize anything.

IF YOU ARE A JOE . . .

You're the quintessential uncle—fat, bald, never married—although your nephews think you're a sloth. You have the reflexes of a garden slug, with a personality to match. You never quite get the joke—primarily because you're most often the butt of it.

IF YOU ARE A CURLY JOE . . .

You're kidding yourself. Seek professional guidance.

Bet You Didn't Know! #14

Moe first spotted Larry in 1925 at a Chicago nightclub called the Rainbow Gardens. Larry was performing a Russian dance while wearing a high hat and tails and playing a violin. Larry was offered $90 a week to join the Stooges . . . and another $10 per week if he'd bury the fiddle.

STILL SHOTS #4

Larry's playing a selection from which popular musical?

A. *Hello, Dummy*

B. *The Music Mangle*

C. *Fiddler on the Skids*

The three favorite Stooges statues—Moe, Larry, and Curly.

How many Stooges does it take to screw in a light bulb? This hard-to-find statue features Shemp as the third wheel.

STATUES

   Plaster busts of the Stooges are a popular item, as many fans display them in their offices and bedrooms. Other fans, we are told, use them as sort of a shrine, at which they sacrifice old Ritz Brothers films each morning as a symbol of strength.

Value

Stooges Statues...............................$55

Where to get them:

   Contact the manufacturer, Esco Products, Inc., or ask at your local tobacco shop, gift shop, or other retail specialty shop.

"Moe Blows His Top" boasts this 1960 gum dispenser. When triggered, a wad of gum actually popped out of Moe's scalp.

STOOGES COLLECTIBLES YOU COULD EAT

No self-respecting candy manufacturer could have witnessed the effect the Stooges were having on children in the early 1960s and not done something about it. The first to cash in on the little appetites was the Phoenix Candy Company, which marketed Candy Taffy Kisses with a Stooges wrapper.

The L. H. Becker company sold a plastic gum dispenser with the Stooges' faces imprinted on it. The novelty was that Moe's scalp popped off whenever you wanted a piece of gum.

Value

Nothing. This stuff is 20 years old! If you want to eat it, that's your problem. Actually, the gum dispenser is worth a few dollars, if for no other reason than the fact that, when the gum ran out, most kids tossed the dispenser away.

Gum Dispenser $3

Where to get it:

This item is hard to find. Your best bet is to contact the Three Stooges Club.

FOOD, FOOD, FOOD

The Stooges were preoccupied with food, both onscreen and off. In fact, while working on the feature film *Have Rocket, Will Travel* (1959), Moe recalled the lengths they would go to just to ensure that the food they threw was the best. "Larry met up with a French chef who taught the property man how to make a bowl of Bourguignon that was out of this world. The trick was to simmer the beef. The best thing about the Bourguignon was that it not only was delicious, but it had a rich consistency perfect for spotting white linen suits and smearing our faces. What memories!"

Curly was famous for his escapades featuring various foodstuffs. He found misery, in one form or another, with the following types of food: submarine sandwiches (one bit him on the nose), lobsters (one bit him on the nose), any form of shelled nut, and, of course, pies.

Speaking of cooking, the Stooges were pretty handy around the kitchen themselves. Remember some of their concoctions? They include a walking turkey (its live-parrot stuffing the cause), hors d'oeuvres made of dog biscuits and a can of peas, a layer cake with one layer actually a throw pillow, a gas-filled cake, and a marshmallow cake with bubble gum in place of marshmallow.

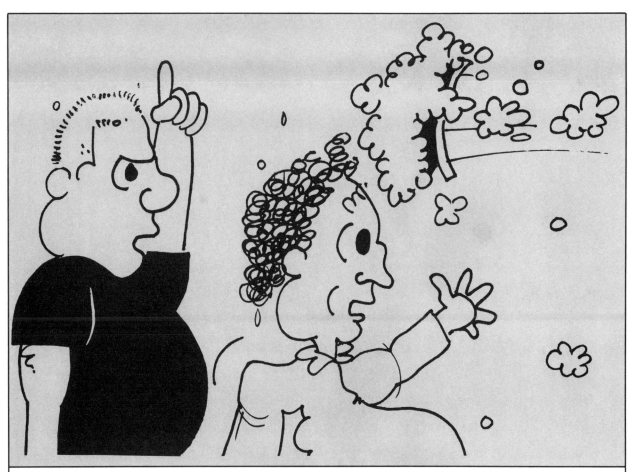

ANATOMY OF A STOOGE PIE

Meticulous performers, the Stooges were adamant over the contents of the pies they tossed, because they eventually wound up wearing them as well. The custard pies the Stooges became famous for tossing were actually not custard at all; custard won't stick to an actor's face. The Stooges' pies usually consisted of a combination of marshmallow, ground pumpkin, molasses, chocolate syrup, ketchup, and huckleberries. Occasionally the Stooges substituted thick fruit filling for one or more ingredients; blueberries, cherries, and strawberries were among the team's favorites. But, as Moe once recalled, by the end of a day's filming, the pies, after having been scraped off the floor and used over and over again, were loaded with sawdust, wood shavings, and even nails left over from the set construction! No wonder the most popular strategy in a Stooges pie fight was ducking!

41. In *Men in Black* (1934), the Stooges run rampant through the corridors of a large city hospital. What is the name of that hospital?

42. *Ants in the Pantry* (1936) casts the Stooges as would-be pest exterminators. What is the name of the company they work for?

43. What song do the Stooges spoof at the finale of *Nutty but Nice* (1940)?

44. Character actor Emil Sitka steals the show in the Stooges' 1952 short subject *Gents in a Jam*, playing the role of Uncle Phineas. In terms of personal wealth, how much is Phineas worth?

45. What is the character name of the devilish temptress in the Stooges' 1955 short subject *Bedlam in Paradise*?

46. What planet do the Stooges journey to in their 1957 short subject *Space Ship Sappy*, featuring Benny Rubin as a screwball scientist?

47. Sonny Bupp played Charles Foster Kane as a child in the screen classic *Citizen Kane* (1941). He also played a child in which Stooge short?

48. Who plays the Stooges' mother in *Cactus Makes Perfect* (1942)?

49. In *Violent Is the Word for Curly* (1938), the boys masquerade as professors. At what college do they entertain?

50. What is the name of the law firm in both *Hold That Lion* (1947) and *Loose Loot* (1953)?

STOOGE MANIA

AUTOGRAPHS

Perhaps the most elusive of all Stooges collectibles, Stooges autographs are the fans' most direct link to the Stooges themselves. And since Shemp and Curly died long before the Stooges found mass adulation, their signatures are much more difficult to obtain than Moe's or Larry's. For a time, Moe's daughter Joan Maurer was selling canceled checks with Moe's signature, the proceeds going to the City of Hope for cancer research. She has reportedly raised some $40,000 for the cause.

Yes, the Stooges knew how to sign their names. And usually on the first try, too. Their autographs—especially Curly's and Shemp's—command a premium price on the signature market today.

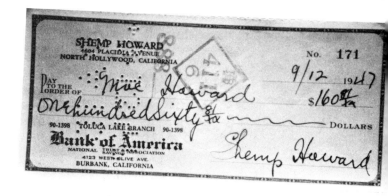

This rare personal check features Shemp's signature, and is made out to Moe.

Joe Besser and Joe DeRita, because they remain approachable to autograph seekers, have slightly less valuable autographs.

Value

Moe Howard	$5
Curly Howard	$100
Shemp Howard	$100
Larry Fine	$5
Joe Besser	$1
Joe DeRita	$1

This page from a fan's scrapbook features a rare photo of the offstage Stooges and an even rarer Curly autograph. Hard to tell they're singing the same song, isn't it?

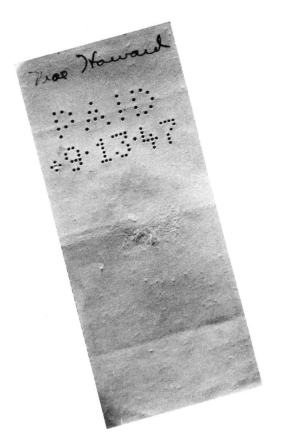

Another source for Stooge autographs—the endorsement found on the back of the check.

This personal letter from Moe Howard reveals that his early 1970s speaking fee was only $1,600. Today he'd barely make plane fare for that price.

Where to get them:

Both Joes reside in North Hollywood, California, and can be contacted there. For signatures of the deceased members, try the Universal Autograph Collector's Club.

ONE WAY TO PROVIDE FOR YOUR FUTURE: STOOGES CURRENCY

In the early 1960s, the Mahana Importing Company issued a Three Stooges Savings Bank. And, to give you something to save, Three Stooges Dollar Bills are actually negotiable currency, with Moe, Larry, and Curly where George Washington used to be. For you high-rollers, a special $2 version is available.

Where to get them:

Try the Three Stooges fan clubs.

#15

The Stooges played in celebrity baseball tournaments throughout their career; in fact, the boys were fairly good athletes, as their physical brand of humor demanded that they be in top shape. In the early 1920s, Moe Howard appeared in 12 two-reel silent sports comedies with none other than the legendary Honus Wagner, considered by many to be the greatest shortstop of all time. And in the 1983 World Series, the Stooges were instrumental in deciding the outcome—Orioles Rick Dempsey, Rich Dauer, and Jose Cruz were dubbed Moe, Larry, and Curly by their teammates for their spirited behavior.

STOOGES MASQUERADE

Three Stooges Halloween costumes and masks were sold by Ben Cooper at the height of the Stooges' popularity (and at only $3 a pop) in 1961. Twenty years later, Nat Cooper is selling latex masks of the Stooges.

Where to get them:

Most costume shops stock one or two of the Stooges masquerade items.

ANATOMY OF A STOOGES FAN

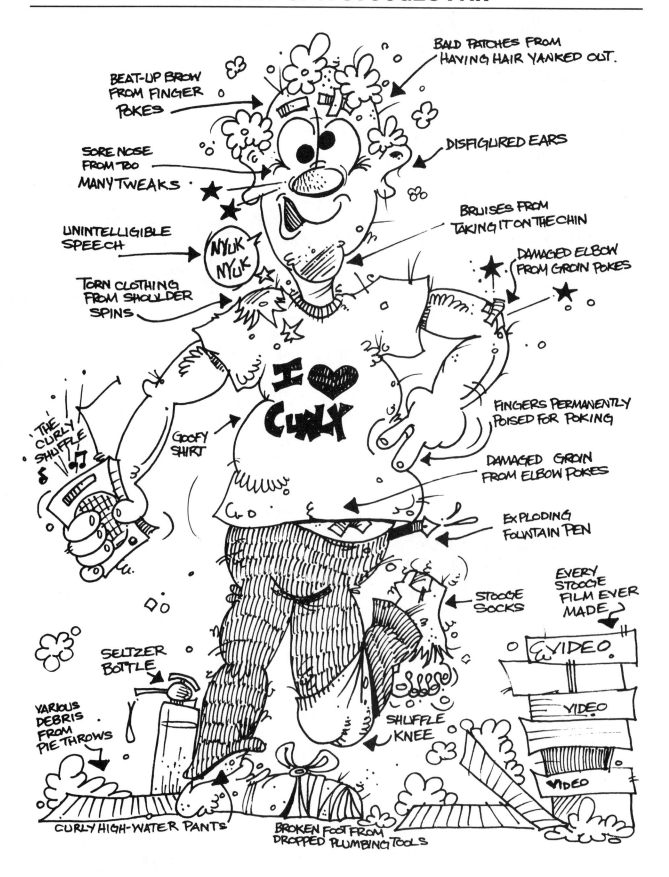

COMIC BOOK STOOGES

One of the most popular Stooges items—and, because of their wide distribution, one of the most plentiful—are Stooges comic books. There are six distinct series known today, spanning some three decades.

Title (publisher/numbers)	Value
The Three Stooges (Jubilee/#1)	$100–125
The Three Stooges (Jubilee/#2)	$75–100

The Jubilee issues are by far the most popular of the Stooges comics. They were issued in 1949 and featured Curly as the third Stooge, even though he had left the team three years earlier.

The two Jubilee issues were actually no more than cartoon versions of the most popular Stooges shorts. The storylines closely followed various Stooges scripts; issue #1 includes an adaptation of the classic Stooges short *Hoi Polloi*.

These first two issues are considered scarce—only 100 copies of each issue are known to exist.

Title (publisher/number)	Value
The Three Stooges (St. John/#1)	$75–100

Jubilee Publications canceled the initial *Three Stooges* series after only two issues. Four years later, in 1953, the Jubilee company changed hands and became the St. John Publishing Company. The series was revived but featured Shemp as the third Stooge. The storylines in this second series were original, if sometimes reminiscent of the shorts. In the first issue, for instance, the story "Bell Bent for Treasure" was actually an adaptation of the 1937 Stooge short *Cash and Carry*.

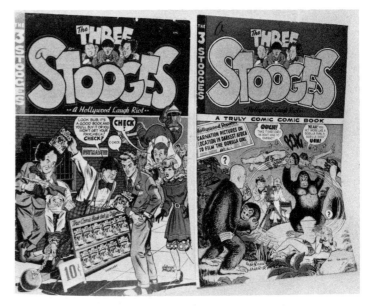

The rarest of the Stooge comic books, issues 1 and 2 of "The Three Stooges" series, were the only comics to feature Curly as the third Stooge.

Title (publisher/number)	Value
The Three Stooges (St. John/#2/#3)	$55–70/$45–60

Issues 2 and 3 of the St. John series followed the pattern set by the premiere issue, with one major exception: the books were printed in 3-D. Only two such issues saw the light of day (at 32 pages, they were half the size of the first St. John issue), and they, too, met with only moderate success.

St. John issues 4–7 marked a return to traditional artwork. Number 7, in October 1954, marked the end of the series.

Issue Number	Value
4	$20–25
5	$20–25
6	$20–25
7	$15–20

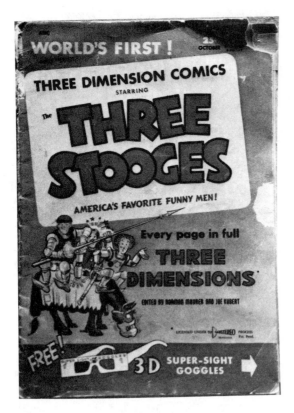

Issues 2 and 3 of St. John's "The Three Stooges" series were really eye-catching—provided you were wearing your 3-D glasses. The comics were unreadable without them.

The Dell Publishing Company capitalized on the Stooges' television popularity by featuring full-color photos of the team on the covers of their comic books. Note the price change; between the issue above and the one at the top of page 93 even then the Stooges could command an extra nickel from the most frugal fan.

As the Stooges entered the television age, their newfound popularity encouraged the Dell Publishing Company to try a third Stooges comic book series, with Curly Joe as the third Stooge. These issues feature full-color photos of the Stooges on the covers, accounting for their continued popularity among collectors.

Issue Number	Value
1	$8–10
2	$8–10
3	$8–10
4	$8–10
5	$8–10
6	$8–10
7	$8–10
8	$8–10
9	$8–10
10	$8–10

Just in case you're interested, Dell issues 1–5 are technically part of the Four-Color series, which Dell discontinued in 1962. The Four-Color issues are listed below:

Dell Issue Number	Four-Color Number
1	1043
2	1078
3	1127
4	1170
5	1187

The "Three Stooges Meet Hercules" issue is actually part of Dell's "Movie Classics" series (#01828-208).

In addition, there is one more known variation—"Three Stooges in Orbit"—which is part of the Gold Key/Whitman series "Movie Comics" (#30016-211).

In 1962, Dell included the Stooges as part of its "Comic Album" series:

Issue #18 . . . . $4–5

Dell formed a separate publishing company—Gold Key—and continued "The Three Stooges" series through issue #55, which was published in 1972. This final Dell series featured several special movie editions, including "The Three Stooges Meet Hercules," "The Three Stooges in Orbit," "The Three Stooges Go Around the World in a Daze," and "The Outlaws Is Coming!" "The Three Stooges in Orbit" was actually comprised of frame blow-ups from the film, with captions. These issues are among the most available of the Stooge comics, and can often be found at comic book shows and conventions.

Issue Number	Value
10	$7–8
11	$7–8
12	$7–8
13	$7–8
14	$7–8
15	$7–9
16	$7–8
17	$7–8
18	$7–8
19	$7–8
20	$7–8
21	$2–4
22	$2–4
23	$2–4
24	$2–4
25	$2–4
26	$2–4
27	$2–4
28	$2–4
29	$2–4
30	$2–4
31	$2–4
32	$2–4
33	$2–4
34	$2–4
35	$2–4
36	$2–4
37	$2–4
38	$2–4
39	$2–4
40	$2–4
41	$2–4
42	$2–4
43	$2–4
44	$2–4
45	$2–4
46	$2–4

"The Three Stooges in Orbit" and "The Three Stooges Meet Hercules" were based on Stooge feature-length films of the same titles.

Issue Number	Value
47	$2–4
48	$2–4
49	$2–4
50	$2–4
51	$2–4
52	$2–4
53	$2–4
54	$2–4
55	$2–4

In the 1960s, Western/Gold Key teamed with K. K. Publications to issue nine comic books in the ongoing "March of Comics" series. These half-size, 16-page issues were distributed to various retailers as an advertising handout. The books featured full-color photos of Stooges Moe Howard, Larry Fine, and Joe DeRita on the covers.

Issue Number	Value
232	$8–10
248	$8–10
268	$7–8
280	$7–8
292	$7–8
304	$7–8
316	$7–8
336	$7–8
373	$4–5

In 1972, as "The Three Stooges" series was discontinued, Gold Key released one final series. The premise—the lives of the Stooges' offspring, involved in wacky escapades just like their fathers—didn't wash. Only seven issues were produced.

Issue Number	Value
1	$1–1.50
2	$.75–1
3	$.75–1
4	$.75–1
5	$.75–1
6	$.75–1
7	$.75–1

Comics featuring color photos of the Stooges remain popular—and available—collectibles. Comic books shown here are from the Dell and Gold Key/Whitman series.

Curly Joe, Moe, and would-be Stooge Emil Sitka laugh at the zany antics chronicled in the Stooges comics.

The Jubilee-issued Stooges comics, along with "The Little Stooges" series published by Gold Key, has a unique connection to the Stooges. The artist and sometime writer for both series was Norman Maurer—husband of Joan Maurer, Moe Howard's daughter. It was Maurer (already an established comic artist when he met future wife Joan) who initially approached the Stooges and eventually capped the deal with Jubilee.

STILL SHOTS #5

"You know something, Porcupine?"

A. "If your forehead was any bigger, we could shoot a western on it."

B. "If you were as dumb as you are ugly, you'd still be smarter than most of your relatives."

C. "Your face reminds me of the economy—your hairline is in recession and your chins are inflated."

CHARACTERISTIC QUOTES #13-18

These lines were taken from actual Stooges shorts. Can you name the speaker and the film the line is from? Of course you can!

13. "I didn't do it! He's the one!"

14. "Let's go to Tunis and have Tunis-salad sandwiches!"

15. "I'm sorry, Moe, I didn't see ya standin' there!"

16. "If the cake in that oven turns out like that turkey, you'll be the next one to broil in it! And I'm gonna baste ya with nitric acid!"

17. "If at first you don't succeed, keep on suckin' 'til ya *do* suck seed!"

18. "I'll tear your tonsils out and tie it around your neck for a bow tie!"

Answers are in the Appendix.

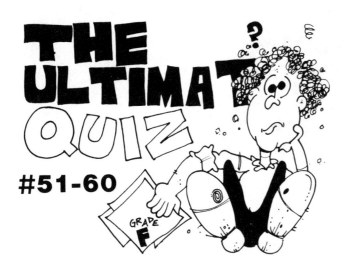

THE ULTIMAT QUIZ

#51-60

GRADE F

51. What is the name of Kenneth MacDonald's character in *Blunder Boys* (1955)?

52. What are the three kinds of cheese used to pacify Curly in *Horses' Collars* (1935)

53. The phrase "Look at the grouse," as heard in "The Curly Shuffle," originated in what Stooges short subject?

54. Which Joe Besser Stooges episode features no supporting players beside the Stooges themselves?

55. Which longtime Stooges supporting player made his Stooge film debut in Curly's last effort, *Half-Wits' Holiday* (1947)?

56. Which Stooges short parodies Tennessee Williams' play, A *Streetcar Named Desire*?

57. Which one of the Stooges actually began in show business as a Shakespearean actor?

58. Which Stooges film features a squeaking bat with Shemp Howard's face?

59. In *Termites of 1938* (1938), the Stooges run their own exterminating business. What's the name of the company?

60. What's the name of the interior decorator whom Moe impersonates in *Tassels in the Air* (1938)?

Former Stooge Joe Besser as he appears today, with wife Ernie.

STOOGE MANIA

COLORING BOOKS

In addition to the comic books, the Stooges appeared in dozens of coloring books, punch-out books, and other publications aimed at kids. Funbuilt Toys issued a series of *Three Stooges Magic Coloring Books* in the early 1960s, marking the first wave of material. Following is a list of coloring books and related material.

Value

Three Stooges Magic Coloring Books	$5
Three Stooges Coloring Books (Lowe, Inc.)	$3
Three Stooges Coloring Book (Whitman)	$3
Three Stooges Punch-out Book (Whitman)	$5
Three Stooges Cut-Out Book (Whitman)	$3
Three Stooges Stamp Book (Whitman)	$8
Three Stooges Sticker Fun Book (Whitman)	$8

Where to get them:

Check the paper-related collectible shops, such as Remember When and Classic Movie and Comic Center.

The Whitman Company cashed in on the Stooges' popularity with a 128-page coloring book officially "authorized" by the team. As with other collectibles produced in the late 1950s and 1960s, the coloring book featured Joe DeRita as the third Stooge.

STOOGEAEROBICS: THE MODERN-DAY WAY TO TRIM INCHES AWAY

Curly's scrambling around was good for something other than floor burns. Now you, too, can use the techniques developed by our Flatbush flathead, simply by following this handy guide. Have yourself a physical fit!

1. Selection of music is essential to generating a feeling of energy and a proper sense of excitement. You may select from any one of the following titles:

    "Listen to the Mockingbird"

    "Three Blind Mice"

    "The Curly Shuffle"

    Or, of course, you can use "Pop Goes the Weasel," which should get you fighting mad.

2. Begin with several knee bends, a quick shuffle, and a few face slaps.

3. As the action heats up, show your excitement with several "woo-woo-woos" and a "nyuk, nyuk" or two.

4. By now you should be dancing furiously in place, feet flying in several directions at once, as your brow becomes redder and redder.

5. Hit the deck! You're ready for the shoulder spin now, in tribute to the world's first breakdancer—Curly.

6. Cool down. Drink a bottle of ink.

GAMES

Colorforms Company joined forces with the Stooges in the early 1960s and released some game-related items.

Value

Three Stooges Silly Riddle Game............$10
Three Stooges Colorforms Set...............$25

Where to get them:

Try Gasoline Alley Antiques or contact collectors through the Stooges fan clubs.

The Empire Plastic Company also released several items, again cashing in on the newfound interest in the Stooges displayed in the early 1960s.

Value

Three Stooges Bowling Set.....................$5
Three Stooges Spinning Top $5

Where to get them:

Try Gasoline Alley Antiques.

The Joe DeRita Fitness Plan, as told to writer Al Steen in 1959: "Go to bed late. Getting up early is for the birds, which get nothing but a worm. Smoke 20 cigars a day. Eat as much as you like, particularly pies, ice cream, and cake. Get a balloon around your middle. Then join up as one of the Three Stooges. The pushing around will keep you physically fit, if it doesn't kill you first."

TEN TERMS YOU WON'T LEARN FROM BERLITZ

1. "Soiteny" (Not Soiten/y)
2. "Why, you . . .!"
3. "Look at the grouse!"
4. "Numbskull!"
5. "Oh, a wise guy!"
6. "I'm a victim of soicumstance!"
7. "Oh, a back-biter, eh?"
8. "Reminds me of the reform school!"
9. "I'll murder ya!"
10. "Moe! Larry! Cheese!"

The Stooges—or reasonable facsimiles thereof—can be found gracing the covers of a variety of magazines (some more appropriately named than others), a tribute to their lasting popularity.

MORE FILM ITEMS

Since the Stooges made their fame in the movies, it's only natural that film-related Stooge merchandise is both plentiful and varied.

Value

Easy Show Projector (Kenner) $30
Three Stooges TV Viewer (Acme Toy Corp.)$10

There was even a Three Stooges Magic Foto Club, which, for $1, would enable anyone to develop autographed photos of the Stooges with the Magic Foto paper and Magic Fixer.

Larry, Moe, and Shemp pose with director Ed Bernds after receiving the Laurel Award for continued box office success.

THE ULTIMATE QUIZ

#61-70

GRADE F

61. What drives Curly to the brink of insanity in *Grips, Grunts, and Groans* (1937)?

62. What is the title of the short subject in which Moe Howard, Larry Fine, and Jerry (Curly) Howard received story credit?

63. Which one of the Stooges was nicknamed "Babe"?

64. Which short subject features Moe as Simple Simon and Larry as Little Miss Muffet?

65. What is the name of Phil Van Zandt's evil character in the Stooges short *Bedlam in Paradise* (1955)?

66. Which Stooges short features Emil Sitka as theatrical producer B. K. Doakes?

67. The Stooges film *Ants in the Pantry* (1936) was later remade as what Stooges short starring Shemp?

68. Which one of the Stooges started his career as an assistant to vaudeville magician Howard Thurston?

69. Which Stooges short features Lucille Ball as a platinum blonde?

70. Which Stooges film features Moe's daughter, Joan, and Larry's daughter, Phyllis, in small roles?

Bet you Didn't Know! #18

Moe Howard used to get his famous bowl haircut trimmed to perfection by a Hollywood barber. The barbershop, located on Vine Street near the Capitol Records Building, still stands. According to Stooges movie foil Emil Sitka, Moe didn't have much trouble convincing his barber to cut it the way he wanted it—Moe owned the business.

STOOGE
MANIA

VINYL TOYS

Now, really, inflatable likenesses of the Stooges? For what? To punch, of course. In 1959, the Van Dam Rubber Company put out a Three Stooges Punching Bag, with a caricature of Moe right where your fist ought to be. The Hampshire Company got in on the action, too, by marketing Three Stooges Inflatable Vinyl Punchos. And Ideal later released inflatable vinyl toys of the Stooges.

Value

Van Dam Punching Bag $50
Hampshire Punchos $10
Ideal Vinyl Toys..............................$5–8

Where to get them:

Better try the Stooges fan clubs. These will be hard to locate.

STILL SHOTS #6

What popular song was inspired by this classic movie scene?
A. "I'm Just Mad about Larry"
B. "Cuddle Up a Little Grosser"
C. "I Lost My Lunch in San Francisco"

STOOGES SCRIPT

Herewith, a portion of *Pardon My Terror,* a proposed Curly short that was never produced with the Stooges. The piece was written by longtime Stooge scripter Edward Bernds. Such never-filmed scripts as this are very rare and command a premium price on the collectors' market. This script has been reproduced to appear like the original, mispellings, corrections, deletions, and all.

STOOGE COMEDY #4068

"PARDON MY TERROR"

By

Edward Bernds

First Draft
March 21, 1946

STOOGE COMEDY

FADE IN: NIGHT

1 EXT. MORTON MANSION (STOCK) LONG SHOT:

A gloomy-looking old house.

2 INT. MORTON LIBRARY LONG SHOT:

An old man - Jonas Morton - is working at a desk.

3 CLOSE SHOT:

From behind a drape, we see the claw-like hands of the strangler emerge.

4 MED. SHOT:

In shadows, we see the silhouette of the strangler creep up on Morton. Suddenly he pounces on him. We hear the crash of the chair and a hoarse yell from Morton.

5 CLOSE SHOT AT DOORWAY:

A pretty girl - Alice Morton - dashes in, having heard the yell. She looks off, horrified, and runs out again, screaming.

6 INT. MORTON LIVING ROOM:

Alice is met by a hard-visaged character - Mr. Grooch - the Mortons' lawyer.

ALICE (hysterically)
Mr. Grooch! Grandfather's been killed! In the library - I saw him! Please come!

She drags Grooch after her into the library. As they leave the scene, a sinister-looking servant, Jarvis, sneaks out of a doorway and looks after them menacingly.

7 INT. LIBRARY MED. SHOT:

As they enter, Alice stares unbelievingly. No one is in the room, and there is no sign of a struggle.

2

7 CONTINUED:

ALICE (at a loss)
He's gone! He was right there! I saw him!

GROOCH (smoothly)
My dear girl -- you're wrought up-- nerves, of course! Why not run out to the country for a few days --

ALICE (interrupting)
I saw him, I tell you!

She picks up the telephone with sudden decision and dials "O".

GROOCH (quickly)
What are you going to do?

ALICE (consulting a card)
Call the detective agency -- hello operator -- State 4724 please --

Grooch reacts to her intentions and takes something from his picket.

8 INSERT: A spring-blade knife - the blade pops out.

9 MED. SHOT:

For a moment we think Grooch is going to stab Alice. Instead he cuts the telephone wire. Alice is unaware of this and reacts as the phone goes dead.

ALICE
--hello --- hello! Operator!

She gives up, slams down the receiver, and starts for the door.

GROOCH
Where are you going?

ALICE (without stopping)
To the detective agency!

She exits.

10 CLOSE SHOT:

Grooch stares after her vindictively. Behind him, Wanda, a sinister-looking, exotic female emerges from the drapes.

4

15 MED. SHOT:

The Stooges look at a radio receiver - the kind that receives code. Curly joins Moe and Larry at the desk.

                    MOE
        It's the secret code! Curly, take
        it down!

Moe and Larry listen tensely as Curly writes. Finally the code ends.

                    MOE
        What did it say?

                    CURLY
        Dot - dit - dit dot - dit - dit!

Moe and Larry, annoyed, begin pounding him. They are interrupted by a knock on the door. The stooges immediately get very busy trying to impress a prospective client. Moe grabs the phone, Larry takes the magnifying glass, and Curly gets busy with some papers. He signs them with a flourish and then drops them in the wastebasket.

                    MOE
        Yes sir, our fee will be five thousand
        dollars -- very well sir, we'll take
        care of it! Wide-Awake -- that's us!

He hangs up and turns to Larry.

                    MOE
        Interesting case, Doctor -- most
        interesting! Murder, you know!

                    LARRY
        Most interesting! We haven't had a
        good murder lately!

In trying to put on a good show, the Stooges have turned their backs to the door, and Dugan, their landlord, enters and glowers at them. He waits until Larry finishes his speech.

                    DUGAN
        ~~INTERRUPTING~~ You will have!

The boys take it when they discover Dugan.

                    MOE
        Oh hello, Mr. Dugan -- I was thinking
        about you just this morning ---

3

10 CONTINUED

                    WANDA
        You fool! Why didn't you stop her?

                    GROOCH
        No - no --- I have a better idea!

He picks up the card.

                    GROOCH (reading)
        Wide-awake Detective Agency ---
        Let them come --- we'll be ready for
        them!

He laughs ghoulishly as we:

                              DISSOLVE TO:

11 INSERT: A sign on a glass door.
             "WIDE AWAKE DETECTIVE AGENCY."

12 INT. DETECTIVE AGENCY OFFICE (NIGHT) MED. SHOT:
    ~~Larry and Moe are busy at a desk. Curly sits in a chair.~~

13 CLOSE SHOT ~~...~~
    Larry is cleaning a big horse-pistol, while Moe is examining a dagger with a huge magnifying glass. Larry drops something, bends to pick it up, and his head moves into Moe's view.

                    MOE (startled)
        Camels!

He discovers his mistake, pulls a handful of Larry's hair out, and examines it more closely with the glass. Larry yells his protest, and Moe casually raps him with the magnifying glass. (prop-rim only)

14 CLOSE SHOT CURLY ...
    He sits, apparently staring straight ahead. Over his closeup, we hear the dot-dash-dot of radio code. He blinks and wakens, and we see that they have "eyes" painted on his closed lids.

6

15 CONTINUED:

                    DUGAN (roaring)
          The word is defectives! Now what about
          my rent!

Moe, at a loss, sees the horse-pistol on the desk. He points
it at Dugan.

                    MOE
          See this gun? I'm gonna let you have
          it!

                    DUGAN
          No! No! Don't shoot!

                    MOE
          Shoot? I ain't gonna shoot! I'm gonna
          give you the gun for collackteral!

                    LARRY
          Yeah - here's mine too!

He pulls a Civil War cavalry pistol out of a drawer and
hands it to Dugan.

                    CURLY
          Yeah -- mine too.

He draws a water-pistol.

                    DUGAN
          Does that thing shoot?

                    CURLY
          Soitenly it shoots!

He pulls the trigger and Moe gets a stream of ink in the
face. Moe burns, but does not retaliate immediately.

                    MOE (to Dugan)
          See? It shoots!

Curly relaxes when he thinks Moe is not going to hit him. Moe
quickly picks up a steel trap and crowns Curly with it.
(rubber strips on the trap) The trap is set, and Moe tosses
it on a chair.

16 CLOSE SHOT DUGAN:

He examines the guns disgustedly.

                    DUGAN
          These guns won't even go off!

He tosses them in the open drawer of the desk.

5

15 CONTINUED:

                    DUGAN
          What about the rent?

                    MOE
          Now that's a good question -- ~~the rent~~--

[handwritten: Did ever tell you the story -- Dugan the rent -- What about the rent]

                    LARRY
          We'll find it somewhere!

                    CURLY
          Sure!

He starts looking with the magnifying glass, getting into
Dugan's pockets before Dugan beats him off.

                    DUGAN
          Get out of here! I want my money!

                    MOE (suddenly dramatic)
          Money! What's money? The root of all evil,
          that's what it is! What do the Indians
          use for money? Wampum! What do the South
          Sea Islanders use? Shells! What do the
          Eskimos use? Fish!

Curly thinks this is very funny, and cackles like a hysterical
hen.

                    MOE (angrily)
          What's so funny?

                    CURLY
          Must be awful messy when an Eskimo
          plays a slot machine!

Moe and Larry give him a good going-over.

                    DUGAN (beside himself)
          This ain't getting the rent paid!
          Who ever told you you were detectives?

                    MOE (aggreived)
          The draft board! They examined us --
          they said: "these men are detectives".
          We got papers to prove it!

He hands some papers to Dugan, who is impressed. He reads,
and his eyes widen. Suddenly he delivers a triple slap
to the boys.

7

17 MED. SHOT:

As the guns land in the drawer, the whole desk blows up. Explosions burst out of every drawer, and the whole desk starts jumping around.

18 CLOSE SHOT MOE:

A bullet parts his hair.

19 CLOSE SHOT LARRY:

A bullet (squib) hits his back.

20 CLOSE SHOT CURLY:

A bullet (flour pellet) ricochets off of his head, leaving a white streak.

21 MED. CLOSE SHOT DUGAN:

A glass door behind him is broken, and an instant later his derby hat is shot off. That's enough for Dugan. He bolts for the doorway, pursued by shots.

22 CLOSE SHOT NEAR DOORWAY:

On his hands and knees, a colored janitor, Sam, peers into the room as the firing ends.

SAM

~~What's all the shootin' about.~~ Is the shootin' over?

One more shot rings out and knocks his hat off. He ducks back, and emerges again, still closer to the floor.

Sam foolin' this time?

No foolin' this time.

MOE

What's the matter, Sam -- ~~did we scare you~~ scared 7

23 CLOSE SHOT STOOGES:

They emerge from refuge behind an office couch.

24 CLOSE SHOT SAM:

SAM

No sir - I ~~wasn't~~ aint scared -- just a mite agitated.

8

25 CLOSE SHOT STOOGES:

MOE

Why be agitated? Did the bullets come close?

26 CLOSE SHOT SAM:

SAM

Well, middlin' close!

He produces a bucket with about thirty bullet-holes in it, spouting water like a sieve.

27 CLOSE SHOT STOOGES:

They react to the bucket.

MOE

Where'd Mr. Dugan go?

28 CLOSE SHOT SAM:

SAM

I dunno, but he'll get there mighty soon!

He begins to pick up broken glass from the doorway.

29 MED. SHOT:

Alice enters.

ALICE

I'm looking for the Wide-Awake Detective Agency.

SAM

Yes'm - this is it - Wide-Awake -- yes'm.

The Stooges, sensing a client, cluster around her as she enters.

MOE

Goodday, Madam, what can we do for you?

ALICE (appealingly)

I need your help.

Curly, much smitten by her, nearly swoons, but Moe straightens him up with a quick kick.

Personal mementos such as this autographed photo from the late Babe Howard's (former wwife of Shemp) collection are highly prized collectibles.

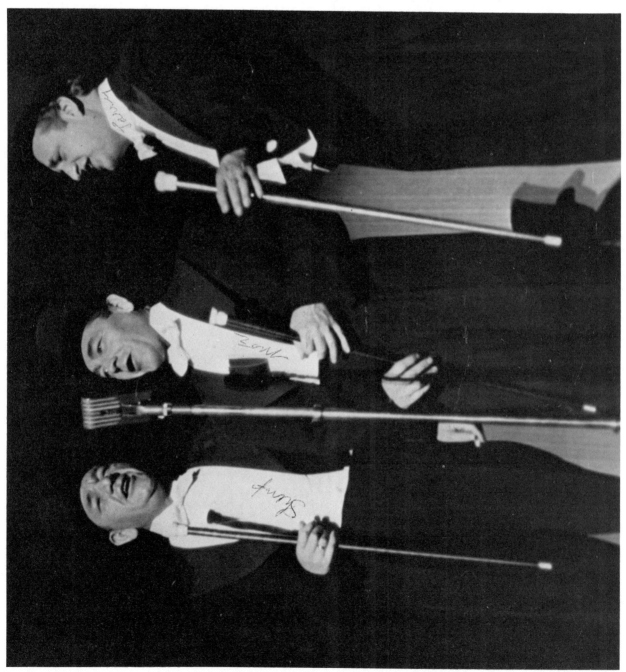

10

33 CONTINUED:

ALICE
Good! Here's the address, and a retainer
fee. (she hands Moe some money) I'll
expect you.

She exits.

MOE
Look at that moola! And there's more
if we find Grandpappy! All right men,
gather the equipment!

34 FULL SHOT:

The Stooges scatter to collect their gear. Curly goes to
a cabinet where the disguises are kept. He tries on one
phoney beard - then decides to take the whole assortment
of wigs, beards and masks. Larry opens a satchel and dumps
in the magnifying glass, a pair of handcuffs, the two pistols
and an inkwell. Moe goes to a corner near the door where he
picks up a camera and a shotgun.

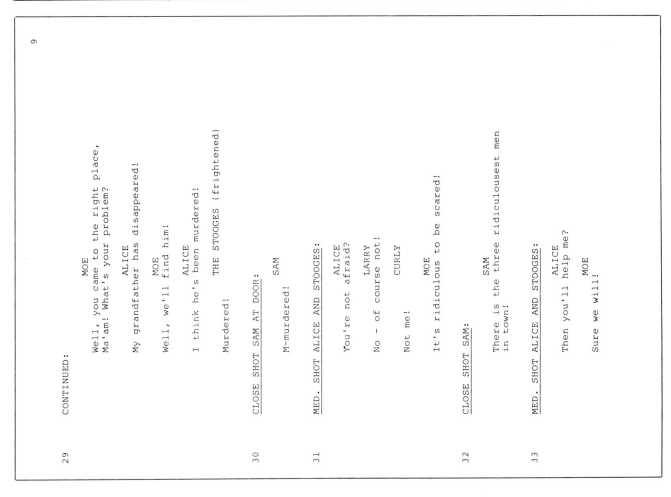

TWO SHOT MOE AND SAM:

MOE
Sam, we'll need some help with this
stuff!

SAM
Don look at me -- no suh!

Moe waves a few bills at him.

SAM
I'm forced to reconsider!

MOE
Good!

He gives Sam the camera and the shotgun.

36 MED. SHOT:

Moe joins Larry and Curly.

MOE
We'll trap that suspect!

CURLY
Oh yeah? I can't find the trap!

MOE
You better find it!

9

29 CONTINUED:

MOE
Well, you came to the right place,
Ma'am! What's your problem?

ALICE
My grandfather has disappeared!

MOE
Well, we'll find him!

ALICE
I think he's been murdered!

THE STOOGES (frightened)
Murdered!

30 CLOSE SHOT SAM AT DOOR:

SAM
M-murdered!

31 MED. SHOT ALICE AND STOOGES:

ALICE
You're not afraid?

LARRY
No - of course not!

CURLY
Not me!

MOE
It's ridiculous to be scared!

32 CLOSE SHOT SAM:

SAM
There is the three ridiculousest men
in town!

33 MED. SHOT ALICE AND STOOGES:

ALICE
Then you'll help me?

MOE
Sure we will!

12

39   <u>INT. CORRIDOR MORTON HOME MED. SHOT:</u>

Jarvis admits Alice.

            ALICE
Jarvis, three men from the detective
agency will be here soon. Please
take care of them.

            JARVIS (with sinister double meaning)
I shall be glad to, Miss Alice.

As Alice exits, Grooch and Wanda, who have been eavesdropping,
join Jarvis.

            WANDA (accusingly, to Grooch)
So! We are to have detectives prying
about!

            GROOCH (craftily)
Ah, but if an accident should happen
to them --

            JARVIS
Please sir, may I be the accident?

He holds up his hands as though to throttle someone.

            WANDA
Jarvis -- have you no finesse? Always
the hands!

She rattles a small bottle with some pills in it.

            WANDA
Look at these -- three little pills --
three little drinks --- three ex-detectives!

            GROOCH
Splendid, my dear -- but see what <u>I</u> have
for them!

He leads the way to a settee and sits upon it.

            GROOCH
Ingenious, don't you think? When that
switch is on (he points) a thousand
volts will crackle through the body
of anyone who sits here!

11

36   CONTINUED:

He bops him, and Curly falls backward into the chair.

37   INSERT: Curly sits on the bear-trap.

38   <u>MED. SHOT:</u>

The trap snaps, and Curly rises with a scream.

            CURLY
I found it!

He turns to show it to Moe.

            DISSOLVE TO:

13

40   CLOSE SHOT JARVIS:

He looks at the switch indicated.

          JARVIS
     This switch, sir?

He throws it.

41   MED. SHOT:

There is a series of flashes under the settee, and Grooch screams as the shock hits him. At last he slides to the floor and breaks the contact. He springs up, ready to murder Jarvis.

          GROOCH
     Why, you idiot --!

He is halted by the ringing of the door chimes.

          WANDA
     The detectives!

Jarvis goes to admit them. Grooch speaks hurriedly to Wanda.

          GROOCH
     We must find out what Alice has told
     them -- with your charms, my dear,
     that should not be difficult!

          WANDA
     Thank you, Phineas!

She rattles the pills meaningly; then Wanda exits as they hear the Stooges enter.

42   INT. CORRIDOR NEAR ENTRANCE DOOR MED. SHOT:

The Stooges enter, loaded down with their props.

          MOE
     Wide Awake Detective Agency, and we
     ain't kiddin', Bud! Say Jeeves --
     where's the corpus delicatessen?

As he speaks, Moe throws the steel trap on Jarvis' foot. As Jarvis howls and bends over, Larry bounces the bag off of his head, and as he straightens up, he bumps his head on the barrel of the gun Curly is carrying. Jarvis is about to wring their necks when Alice and Grooch enter.

14

CONTINUED:

42

          ALICE
     I'm so glad you came! Gentlemen,
     this is Mr. Brooch, our attorney.
     These men are going to help us find
     Grandfather.

          GROOCH (smoothly)
     Oh, really! Well then, I suppose
     You'll want to search for clues.
     Would you rather start where the
     ghostly white figures were seen or
     where we found the pool of blood?

Curly moans, and tries to leave, but Moe and Larry pull him back.

          MOE (frightened but game)
     Oh, we'll just mosey around and look
     the place over -- seeing we're new
     here.

          GROOCH
     Very well. It will be nice -- having
     new blood in the house. (Grooch and
     Alice start to leave. Grooch turns
     back) Please be careful. It's so
     hard to get the blood stains out of the
     rugs!

The boys double-take it as they realize what Grooch means. This time Larry and Curly try to get away, but Moe drags them back.

          MOE
     Come on - come back here! There's
     nothing to worry about if we work
     together! Now look -- we'll spread
     out -- and if one of you gets in a
     tight spot just say "It's warm in
     here". That's our code -- get it? If
     you need help: "It's warm in here".

          LARRY
     Yeah, I get it.

          MOE (to Curly)
     Do you get it?

16

45   CLOSE SHOT CURLY:

He feels that he is being watched. He attempts to tiptoe, but his shoes squeak loudly. He tries to "shush" them. He takes a few more steps; then, feeling the eyes upon him, he looks suddenly at the picture.

46   CLOSE SHOT AT WALL:

The picture swings into place.

47   CLOSE SHOT CURLY:

He examines the picture with his magnifying glass, and then tries to move the picture. It refuses to move. He sings to himself to keep up his courage, and we hear the words "it's warm in here".

48   INT. MORTON LIBRARY MED. CLOSE SHOT MOE:

Moe is tapping for secret panels. He gives a distinctive knock, then moves on a little farther and repeats it. This time the knock is answered. He takes it, and tries again.

49   INT. MORTON LIBRARY CLOSE SHOT LARRY:

Larry reacts as he hears the knock. He answers it, then works his way forward.

50   INT. LIBRARY MED. SHOT:

An offset wall makes an "L" in the library. Moe taps his way down one wall while Larry taps his way down the other. When they come to the point of the "L" they peer cautiously around it! Seeing each other face to face, they scream and run out.

51   INT. LIVING ROOM CLOSE SHOT CURLY:

With his magnifying glass he begins to look for clues. He goes to the floor, examining the carpet as he crawls. The camera pans with him, and suddenly it discloses a shapely ankle in his path. Curly examines it incredulously -- then breathes on his magnifying glass, polishes it and looks again. Finally, convinced it really is an ankle, he rises.

15

42   CONTINUED:

                    CURLY
          What?

Moe bats him.

                    MOE (with pantomine)
          Listen, Marblehead -- a monster has
          me by the throat. He's slowly
          choking me to death! I struggle --
          I get weak -- I'm dying! With my
          last gasp I say "It's warm in here!"
          What do you do?

                    CURLY
          I open the window!

Moe takes the gun away from him and advances on Curly to slug him.

                    CURLY (backing up)
          It's warm in here!

                    MOE (Pleased)
          Oh - you did catch on!

                    MOE
          All right now -- spread out.

He turns away; Curly drops his guard and Moe without looking hits him with the prop gun.

The boys separate. Moe, carrying the gun, goes to the library, Larry to the/study, and Curly to the living room.
                              library

43   INT. MORTON LIVING ROOM MED SHOT:

Curly sneaks in, his shoes squeaking loudly.

44   CLOSE SHOT AT WALL:

A picture moves aside, and through a narrow slit a pair of eyes watches Curly.

52 TWO SHOT CURLY AND WANDA:

WANDA (yearningly)
You have come to save me -- I knew you would!

CURLY
Who, me?

WANDA
I dreamed that a dark, handsome man would come for me!

CURLY (turning to look)
What's keepin' him?

WANDA
Darling!

She embraces Curly.

CURLY
O-oh! It's warm in here!

He means it -- but it reminds him of the code. He repeats it, more loudly.

CURLY
It's warm in here!! Warm!!

WANDA
Come sit down -- after a while, when we've talked, we'll have a little drink. (She leads him to a divan with end arms, and forces him to sit down.) Just let me run my fingers through your hair!

She rubs his head to the accompanying sound effect of sandpaper.

WANDA
What lovely, wavy skin!

Curly reacts and tries to edge away. Wanda pulls him back roughly and puts her arms around him.

CURLY (panicky)
It's warm in here!

WANDA
Why do you keep saying: "it's warm in here?"

52 CONTINUED:

CURLY (loudly)
Because it's warm in here -- and I ain't kidding!

WANDA
Oh, come -- we'll have a little drink together. I have just the thing to cool off!

As she speaks, she pours drinks from a decanter on a table in front of them.

CURLY
Say, I better not. I might get the habit!

Wanda furtively drops a couple of the pills into Curly's drink.

WANDA
Don't worry -- you won't, ~~dream man!~~

CURLY
I won't?

WANDA
Not a chance! Go ahead - drink it, dream man!

She is so ardent that Curly, edging away from her, falls off the end of the divan and his drink spills. Wanda is momentarily angry, but covers up.

WANDA
I'll fix you another one!

She starts to pour another drink. Curly looks at the spilled drink and reacts to what he sees.

53 INSERT: The glass and the spilled drink. The pills, in the wet spot are smoking.

54 TWO SHOT CURLY AND WANDA:

WANDA (handing him another glass)
This will straighten you right out!

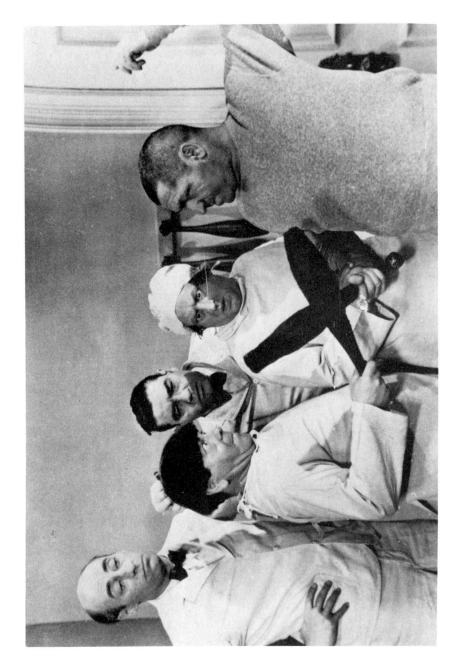

The original Three Stooges Club holds its first meeting.

19

54   CONTINUED:

Curly takes the drink fearfully, and while Wanda is occupied replacing the top of the decanter, he pours it around the base of a potted plant near the divan.

55   INSERT: The plant promptly droops and dies.

56   CLOSE SHOT CURLY:

Curly reacts as he sees the plant die, and rises with a yell.

57   MED. SHOT PANNING:

Curly dashes to a door and throws it open. There, glowering at him, is Grooch. Curly screams and runs to another door.

58   LONG SHOT:

Curly (double) is so frightened he pulls the door open and then crashes into it instead of going through. He recovers and crawls out.

59   INT. CORRIDOR MED. SHOT:

Curly crawls out of the living room, scrambles to his feet, and dashes into the library.

             CURLY (yelling)
    Moe! Larry! It's awful warm! Moe!
    Larry!

60   INT. LIBRARY MED. SHOT:

Moe runs to Curly as he bursts into the room, and Larry enters to join them.

             MOE
    What's the matter, kid?

             CURLY
    Where were you when it was warm in
    there?

20

60   CONTINUED:

             MOE
    It was warm in here too!
    (he gets dramatic)
    I'm lookin' for clues. I hear a
    knock!

             LARRY
    Me too!

             MOE
    I creep forward!

             LARRY
    Me too!

             MOE
    I look around the corner --

             LARRY (eagerly)
    Yeah - me too!

             MOE
    I look right into an ugly puss!

             LARRY
    Boy was he ugly!

Moe and Larry look at each other and yell with sudden recognition. Moe then gets angry and cuffs Larry.

             MOE
    I knew it was you all the time!

             CURLY
    Moe, listen! I nearly got straightened
    out -- with a lily on my chest! A
    dame tried to poison me! I wanta get
    out of here!

             MOE
    No! We get a good hunk of cash if we
    find Grandpappy, and we're going to
    find him! What are you guys, mice?

             LARRY (blustering)
    Wait a minute -- what do you mean!
    (meekly) Yes.

21

60   CONTINUED:

CURLY (also blustering)
Now look here -- ! (meekly) Me too!

MOE (glaring at them)
All right! Let's have a bite to eat and get to work!

He pulls out a slab of Swiss Cheese, bites off a chunk and hands the rest to Larry and Curly.

61   CLOSE SHOT CURLY:

Chewing on his cheese, he notices a plate on a table near him. He squints at it with his magnifying glass.

CURLY
Aha! Aha!

MOE (excited)
Fingerprints?

CURLY
Raspberry jam!

Moe, seemingly impressed, takes the plate from him.

MOE
Remarkable, Bloodhound!

Suddenly Moe smashes the plate (breakaway) on Curly's head.

MOE
Go on! Find some real clues! Get busy!

Curly exits toward a section of bookshelves while Moe and Larry busy themselves elsewhere.

62   INSERT; A peep-hole opens up and a pair of eyes glare out at the boys.

63   CLOSE SHOT CURLY:

He goes to the wall with the bookshelves on it. He removes three or four books, and a fist with a boxing-glove on it comes out of the opening and punches him. Curly reacts, slams the books back, and thinks it over. He takes the books out once more, bending low, and cautiously raises up to look. As soon as his head is in range, the gloved fist lets him have it again.

22

64   ANOTHER ANGLE CURLY AND BOOKSHELVES:

Curly burns again, and this time decides to play it smart. He takes the books out, standing away from the opening. Nothing happens, and he reaches into the opening with his hand. Suddenly the books are pushed aside, creating an opening next to Curly's head, and he gets another punch in the jaw. Curly goes into a dither, screaming with rage.

65   MED. SHOT:

Moe and Larry enter.

MOE
What's the racket, lamebrain?

CURLY
The bookcase keeps hittin' me!

LARRY (to Moe)
Oh, the bookcase keeps hittin' him!

MOE
Why, you dope! How could a bookcase hit you?

CURLY
You try it -- just pull out those books -- go ahead -- try it!

Curly puts Moe in position, and Moe, exasperated, pulls out the books Curly indicates. Nothing happens, and Moe peeps into the space, while Curly waits expectantly. Suddenly the fist comes out of a new place and belts Curly again. Curly howls with rage and pain.

MOE
Oh, I suppose the bookcase hit you again!

CURLY
Yes!

MOE
It did? Like this? (he bops him)

CURLY
Yeah!.

LARRY
And like this? (he hits him)

24

66 CONTINUED:

JONAS

So they were. It had to look good to fool that scoundrel, Grooch! He wouldn't dare show his crooked hand if he didn't think I was dead!

Jonas starts to leave the secret passage.

JARVIS

Where are you going, Sir?

JONAS

I want to keep an eye on Alice. I wouldn't put it past that crook, Grooch, to harm her!

He exits, followed by Jarvis.

67 INT. PARLOR MED. SHOT:

The Stooges enter and listen for sounds of pursuit.

MOE

Well, we're in a fine mess!

LARRY

How are we gonna get out of this place?

CURLY

Oh, they'll just carry us out --- o-o-oh -- what am I saying?

MOE

Shut up! I'll conceive a plan.

He snaps his fingers and pulls a couple of phoney beards from his pocket.

MOE

I got it! I'll disguise myself! Guard that door!

He exits as Larry and Curly watch the door.

68 CLOSE SHOT AT MIRROR:

Moe enters and locks at himself in the mirror. He looks at two false beards, selects one, and puts the other on a table in front of the mirror. He puts on the one he selected, and turns to show the boys.

23

65 CONTINUED:

CURLY (pleased)

Yeah! Just like that!

MOE (another hit)

Not like that?

CURLY

No.

CURLY

Like that!

Just then two gloves come out and wallop Moe and Larry.

The Stooges run to the door and pile out into the corridor.

66 INT. SECRET PASSAGE MED. CLOSE SHOT:

This is a closet-like room behind the bookshelves. Jarvis, with boxing gloves on, is peering out after the departing Stooges. Beside him is Jonas Morton, very much alive.

JONAS

There! That should persuade those meddlers to get out of my house!

JARVIS

Yes sir -- it should indeed, Mr. Morton!

JONAS

If that doesn't get rid of them, we shall have to be more drastic! Why did Alice have to call them in?

JARVIS

After all, sir - she did think you were murdered!

JONAS

We were rather convincing, weren't we, Jarvis? You needn't have been quite so realistic. (he grimaces) My neck is still sore!

JARVIS

Sorry, sir -- your orders were to make it look convincing.

26

71   CONTINUED:

Curly cringes from her, and Moe and Larry try to make an impression on her.

MOE
How do you do, Miss. Don't mind our friend here.

LARRY
He's shy --

MOE
--of brains. Won't you sit down?

WANDA (graciously)
Thank you.

She is about to sit when she remembers that the settee is wired.

WANDA
Oh, thank you, but I must be running along.

She leaves hurriedly.

GROOCH
Now then, if you will be seated ---

The Stooges are about to comply, and have almost made contact when Alice approaches. Again the Stooges spring to their feet.

ALICE
Oh, I've been looking for you. Please come to the library. I have something to show you.

LARRY
Why sure!

MOE (to Grooch)
See you later, Pal.

They exit with Alice. Luke peeps around the corner, sees that the coast is clear, and joins Grooch.

LUKE
Tough luck, boss. You almost had them!

GROOCH
The switch is on -- in one more second they would have fallen into my trap!

25

68   CONTINUED:

MOE
Snappy, eh?

While Moe's back is turned, the glass part of the mirror swings back, leaving the frame, and Luke's head appears. He takes the remaining beard from the table and puts it on, so that when Moe turns back, he is looking at a reasonable facsimile of himself. Moe strokes the beard; Luke does the same. Moe inspects his profile; so does Luke. Moe bends forward; Luke sees so until their noses almost touch. Luke follows every move Moe makes. Finally Moe pulls the whiskers down under his chin; Luke does the same. Moe is puzzled. He breathes on the glass then attempts to rub it with his hand. As he rubs Luke's features he lets out a yell and tears out. Luke vainly tries to grab him through the opening.

69   INT. CORRIDOR MED. SHOT:

As the Stooges emerge, they nearly run into Grooch.

GROOCH
Here you are! I've been looking for you!

MOE
Yeah? We've been looking for a way out!

GROOCH
Sit down, please. I have something important to tell you. Do sit down!

70   INSERT: Grooch's hand closes the switch for the electrified settee.

71   MED. SHOT:

The boys yield to Grooch's urging and are about to sit on the settee. Just then Wanda appears, and the boys straighten up again.

WANDA (to Curly)
Dream boy! Why did you run away?

28

75   CLOSE SHOT ALICE:

She watches them go. Behind her, as she turns to replace
the picture, the bookcase pivots, and out of the opening
a pair of hands (Luke's) emerges. The hands grab Alice,
and she is jerked back into the secret panel.

76   INT. BEDROOM MED. SHOT:

The Stooges enter with Jarvis.

                    JARVIS

          Your quarters, gentlemen. I trust
          you will be comfortable -- but I
          doubt it.

                    MOE

          W-why?

                    JARVIS (impressively)

          After all -- this was the master's
          room. If he was murdered, I'm sure
          his spirit is somewhere about. Good-
          night -- pleasant dreams.

He exits and locks the door. When the Stooges hear the
key turn, they rush to the door and vainly try to open it.

                    MOE

          Trapped like rats!

                    CURLY

          Wait a minute! Don't call me a rat!
          I'm a mouse, remember?

                    MOE

          All right, mousie, try to figure a
          way out of this jam!

Curly exits while Moe and Larry busy themselves with the
door.

77   CLOSE SHOT CLOSET:

Curly enters and opens the closet door, still looking back
at Larry and Moe. In the closet, rigid and pale, is the
"body" of Jonas Morton. Curly screams with fright when
he discovers the body and slams the door.

27

71   CONTINUED:

                    LUKE

          Too bad!

                    GROOCH

          I'll get them!

In deep thought, Grooch and Luke sit down together. Sparks
fly beneath the settee and the two men yell as the voltage
hits them.

72   INT. LIBRARY MED. SHOT:

The Stooges and Alice enter. Alice takes a photograph from
the bookcase.

                    ALICE

          I wanted you to see a picture of my
          grandfather so that you'd know him if
          you found him.

73   INSERT: A picture of Jonas Morton.

74   MED. SHOT:

Moe hands the picture back to her.

                    MOE

          OK - we'll know him.

Jarvis enters.

                    ALICE

          It's rather late now -- if you'd like
          to turn in, Jarvis will show you to
          your room.

                    JARVIS

          Walk this way, please.

He struts off. The Stooges watch him, shrug, and then walk
off, imitating him.

29

77.   CONTINUED:

                    CURLY
          Moe! Moe! A corpus! Right in here!

78.   THREE SHOT THE STOOGES:

Moe and Larry run in.

                    MOE
          What's the matter, kid?

                    CURLY
          Grandpappy's in there - stiff!

                    MOE
          At his age? He oughta be ashamed of
          himself --- you mean --- stiff?

                    CURLY
          Yeah!

                    MOE (timorously)
          All right men, stand back (he shoves
          Curly and Larry in front of him) I'm
          gonna open that door! (he bats Larry)
          Go on, open it!

Larry opens the door. The closet is empty. Moe slams the
door angrily.

                    MOE
          Oh, so grandpappy is in there, eh?
          I'll Grandpappy you!

While Moe is busy giving Curly the works the door opens
silently, and there is Jonas Morton again.

                    MOE (with a glance at Jonas)
          How do you like a guy like that!

The three Stooges do a late take, scream, and run out of
the scene.

79.   CLOSE SHOT AT WINDOW:

As the boys approach the window, the shade flies up with
a clatter, and there, glaring at them, is Luke. The boys
do an about face and rush for the corridor door.

30

60.   MED. SHOT AT DOOR:

The boys rush in. The door is still locked.

                    MOE
          Break it down!

The camera pans with them as they back up for a flying start.

81.   CLOSE SHOT THE DOOR:

It swings open, unassisted.

82.   MED. SHOT PANNING:

The Stooges put their heads down, and make a run for the
door. They go through the open doorway, and we hear a
series of offstage crashes.

83.   INT. CORRIDOR MED. SHOT:

The Stooges have landed in a heap, along with a chair, a
broken vase, and a picture. Moe and Larry recover first
and tear out of the scene toward the living room. Moe,
with the picture-frame around his neck, is groggy, and
staggers out in the opposite direction, toward the parlor.

84.   INT. LIVING ROOM MED. SHOT:

Larry and Curly dash in and begin to barricade the door
against possible pursuit.

85.   INT. PARLOR MED. SHOT:

                                   runs
Moe ~~crashes~~ in. A man is bent over a table examining
something. Moe taps him on the shoulder.

                    MOE
          Hey, Bud, you better be careful --

It is Morton. He stiffens into his corpse attitude, and
Moe, frightened, runs out. Morton quickly follows him.

86 INT. LIVING ROOM MED. SHOT:

The door begins to bulge as someone tries to force his way in. Alarmed, Larry and Curly grab vases (breakaway) and get ready to deal with the intruder. Too late, they see it is Moe, and let him have the vases as he comes through.

87 THREE SHOT STOOGES:

Larry and Curly haul Moe to his feet.

                    LARRY
Sorry, Moe - we didn't know it was you.

                    MOE (with phony forgiveness)
Of course you didn't.

Suddenly he hits them.

                    MOE
If you had, you'd have used iron ones! You numbskulls.

He drives them back until they upset a screen. It falls, disclosing Alice, bound and gagged in a chair.

                    MOE
Hey! What goes on?

The boys hasten to free her.

88 CLOSE SHOT ALICE:

Moe gets the gag off first.

                    ALICE
Thank goodness you found me! We've got to hurry - Grooch is going to steal grandfather's will - I heard him say so!

                    MOE
Why, the dirty crook!

89 CLOSE SHOT AT DOOR:

Morton eases in, listening to Alice's story.

                    ALICE'S VOICE (O.S.)
Grooch and Luke have gone to the library to force the safe!

Morton exits toward them.

90 MED. SHOT:

Morton joins the group.

                    MORTON
They have? We'll trap them there!

                    MOE
Darn right we will! We'll --

The three Stooges do a teriffic delayed take when they realize the "corpse" is talking to them.

                    ALICE
Grandfather! You're alive!

She rushes to his arms.

                    MOE
Y-you are?

                    MORTON
Of course I am! I played possum to smoke out that skunk Grooch, and it worked! In the library, you say? Come on, we'll get him there!

                    MOE (with a gulp)
Will we?

                    MORTON
Of course we will -- because I'll give you twenty-five thousand dollars if you do!

Moe looks at Larry and Curly. All are frightened.

                    MOE
Well, twenty-five grand will buy lots of cheese, mousies --- let's go!

                    ALICE
You're brave men! I can see that!

                    MOE
Lady, you need glasses.

The boys exit.

33

91 INT. CORRIDOR MED. SHOT:

The boys go to the door of the library and go into a quick huddle. Moe and Larry then take stations beside the door, each wielding like a club a prop gun taken from a pair of trophies in the corridor. Curly goes into the library.

92 INT. LIBRARY FULL SHOT:

Luke is attempting to open the safe, making considerable noise. Wanda stands close to him - Grooch some distance farther. Curly enters and approaches Grooch.

93 TWO SHOT CURLY AND GROOCH:

Curly taps him on the shoulder. When Grooch turns Curly chucks him under the chin, makes a gruesome face and runs out with Grooch in pursuit.

94 INT. CORRIDOR MED. SHOT:

The ambush works perfectly. As Grooch emerges, Moe and Larry conk him, and Grooch goes down like a log.

                    MOE
          Nice decoy, egghead! Set 'em up
          in the other alley!

Curly goes back into the library.

95 INT. LIBRARY MED. SHOT:

Luke and Wanda have not noticed Grooch's absence. Curly approaches Wanda, taps her shoulder, and then ogling her coyly, lures her into following him.

96 INT. CORRIDOR MED. SHOT:

Curly comes through the door, but Wanda stops just short of the doorway, and Moe and Larry conk each other. Wanda takes in the situation and runs back for Luke. Curly tries to revive Moe.

                    CURLY
          Moe - Moe -- open your eyes!

34

96 CONTINUED:

                              MOE (looking at him)
               You're beautiful!

                    CURLY
          Boy, is he in bad shape!

97 INT. LIBRARY CLOSE SHOT AT SAFE:

Luke is working on the safe with a sledge hammer. Wanda rushes in.

                    WANDA
          Luke! The detectives! Get them!

Luke drops the sledge in the middle of the room as he goes to the door.

98 INT. CORRIDOR MED. SHOT:

Curly yammers with fear and takes off down the hall. Luke follows him as he dashes into the study.

99 INT. STUDY MED. SHOT:

Curly enters and hides behind the door. As Luke enters and looks around, Curly picks up a chair (breakaway) and smashes it over Luke's head. Luke only shakes his head and makes a grab for Curly.

100 INT. CORRIDOR MED. SHOT:

Curly emerges from the study and runs back to Moe and Larry, who still lie near the library door. Luke is close on his heels, so Curly retreats into the library.

101 INT. LIBRARY MED. SHOT:

Luke corners Curly near the bookshelves and begins to throttle him. Suddenly the gloved fist pops out and jars Luke. He growls in annoyance, but goes back to work on Curly. Again the glove hits him. Luke is enraged, but won't let Curly go. A third blow rocks Luke, and he drops Curly and begins pulling books out in a frenzied effort to find his tormentor.

35

102 CLOSE SHOT CURLY:

Recovering from the choking, he picks up the sledge and swings it.

103 MED. SHOT:

He bongs Luke twice, with seemingly no effect. The third time the sledge handle breaks - and still Luke stays on his feet.

104 CLOSE SHOT LUKE:

We see that his eyes are glassy. Suddenly the glove shoots out and pops him right on the jaw.

105 MED. SHOT:

Luke hits the floor for the count. The secret panel swings open and Morton and Alice emerge. Morton has the gloves on.

ALICE

You did it!

MORTON

The money is all yours!

He reaches back into the panel and brings out packets of greenbacks. Suddenly they freeze.

WANDA'S VOICE (O.S.)

Don't move, anyone!

106 CLOSE SHOT WANDA:

She stands in the doorway, gun in hand. Suddenly a hand comes from behind her and grabs the gun. We see then that Jarvis has the gun and holds Wanda prisoner.

107 MED. SHOT:

MORTON

Good work, Jarvis! A clean sweep, eh!

36

108 CLOSE SHOT CURLY:

He is counting the money, pop-eyed.

CURLY

Look at the dough! We're rich! Moe - Larry!

He runs toward the corridor.

109 EXT. CORRIDOR MED. SHOT:

Moe and Larry are picking themselves up as Curly runs out.

CURLY

Look! I got the dough! We're rich!

110 THREE SHOT THE STOOGES:

Moe and Larry grab packets of the money and riffle it delightedly.

MOE AND LARRY

Hot dog! We're in clover! Boy - oh boy --- look at that dough!

Congratulating themselves, they go to the hot-seat settee.

MOE (just before they sit)

You know something? We're sittin' pretty!

111 LONG SHOT (undercrank):

The boys sit down. Sparks erupt under the seat, and the Stooges shriek as the electricity hits them. They toss their money into the air and run out at top speed. The money continues to filter down like a snowstorm as we

FADE OUT

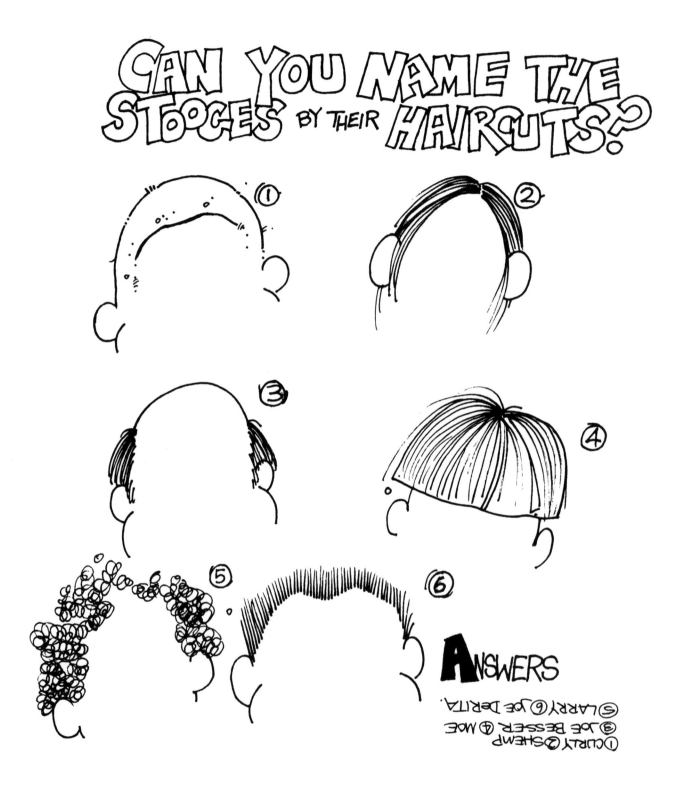

GREETING CARDS

There are currently several versions of Stooges greeting cards and postcards on the market, featuring photos of the Stooges. The legitimate issues are licensed by Columbia Pictures.

Popular Stooges greeting cards feature stills from various shorts.

Value

They're worth only their retail prices right now, but hang on to them; they'll probably appreciate nicely in the future.

Photo 91

Where to get them:

Ludlow Sales exclusively produces the Stooges postcards. They're available in souvenir and gift stores everywhere.

WEBSTER MEETS THE STOOGES

1. **KWAUGH! KWAUGH!** (Kwə Kwə) A gorillalike snort, produced in the back of the throat, used to scare off assorted antagonists.

2. **OH—WO—WO—WO—WO!** (Ō′ wō wō wō wō) Indicates pain, such as that which results from having an anvil dropped on one's foot.

3. **HMMMMMMMMM!** (Hmmmmmmmmmm′) A guttural sound indicating frustration. Usually accompanied by some form of self-flagellation.

4. **NGAAH—AAH—AAH!** (Ngä Ngä) A strangely lilting noise, uttered in recognition of impending doom.

5. **RUFF! RUFF!** (Rəf′ Rəf) The bark, often used as a way of saying, "Oh, yeah?" to some adversary.

6. **NYUK—NYUK—NYUK—NYUK!** (Nyək′ Nyək Nyək Nyək) Usually a display of smug delight.

7. **LA DEE DEE, LA DEE DEE!** (Lä Dē Dē Lä Dē Dē) Sung in a falsetto, this is a way of passing time while completing some menial task—like shaving a block of ice.

8. **WOO-WOO-WOO-WOO-WOO-WOO!** (Wü Wü Wü Wü Wü Wü) Indicates everything from delight to terror.

9. **OBBLOE-OBBLOE-OBBLOE-OBBLOE!** (Ōbŭlō Ōbŭlō Ōbŭlō Obŭlō) The Turkey Yell, usually an indication of sexual excitement.

10. **EEE BEE EEE BEE EEE BEE EEE BEE EEE BEE!** (Ēbēēbēēbēēbēēbē) Inhaled, often used to indicate paralyzing fear or anxiety.

WHAT'S LEFT?

A smattering of memorabilia from the bottom of our treasure chest:

- Three Stooges Hats, issued by the Clinton Toy Company, are virtually extinct now, most likely due to the rough treatment they received from youngsters 20 years ago.
- Three Stooges Stuffed Dolls, by the Juro Novelty Company, were marketed in late 1959.
- There was even Three Stooges Nutty Putty, though it's most likely hard and brittle by now.
- Highly sought as collectibles are the Three Stooges Mugs, produced in 1961, made of ceramic. Fans like to display their mugs around the office.
- A slightly less desirable item is the Three Stooges School Bag, which, along with Stooge loose-leaf binders, made its way into schools around 1962. Carry-Case Manufacturing produced them.
- Kenner, in 1963, issued the Three Stooges Water Color Paint sets, which, by now, are virtually useless, save the Stooges packaging.
- For the truly fashion-minded, Three Stooges Flicker Action Rings (1959) still brighten any wardrobe.

Three Stooges Flicker Action Rings were amusing—if not exactly luxurious—fashion accessories.

Value

Three Stooges Hats	$10
Stuffed Dolls (Juro)	$25
Three Stooges Nutty Putty	$3
Three Stooges Mugs	$25
Three Stooges School Bag	$5
Three Stooges Binders	$3
Water Color Paint Set	$10
Flicker Rings	$8

THREE STOOGES LICENSEES

Following are the manufacturers of Stooges-licensed items, and their products. Check the toy and variety stores in your town; work with them in window and counter displays, in co-op advertising, printed handout material, contest prizes, etc. Listed with the items are retail prices. Wholesale prices can be figured at about 40% discount. Write to the licensees and make arrangements to use the items for lobby sale, as give-aways, contest and lucky door prizes

Allison Mfg. Co.
350 Fifth Ave.
New York, N. Y.
Cotton Knit Tee-Shirts — $1.00

Clinton Toy Corp.
1015 Clinton Stret
Hoboken, N. J.
Hats made of plastic — $ .29

Colorforms, Inc.
Walnut Street
Norwood, N. J.
Vinyl plastic activity sets.
Boxed jigsaw puzzles, color by pencil
sets, rubber stamp sets. — $1.00 and $2.00

Dell Publishing co.
750 Third Ave.
New York 17, N. Y.
Comic Books — $ .10

Ben Cooper, Inc.
200 Fifth Ave.
New York 10, N. Y.
Masks — $ .29
Costumes — $3.00

Empire Plastic Corp.
14 Pelham Parkway
Pelham Manor, N. Y.
Bowling Set, Knock-Em-Down Set.
$1.00 and $2.00
Action Cane — $ .49

Frank M. Fleer Corporation
10th and Somerville
Philadelphia 41, Penn.
Printed Trading Cards with Bubble Gum
$ .05 pkg.

Fun-Bilt Toys, Inc.
1523 South La Cienega
Los Angeles 35, California
Color & Re-Color Books, Cards & Slates
$ .29

Lowell Toy Mfg. Corp.
43-34 37th Street
Long Island City, N. Y.
Boxed Board Games — $2.98

Kenner Products Co.
912 Sycamore St.
Cincinnati, Ohio
Film Strips — $ .25

Smethport Specialty Co.
Smethport, Pa.
Magnetic Toy — $ .79

Golden Records
(A. A. Records, Inc.)
45 Rockefeller Plaza
New York 10, N. Y.
Children's Plastic Phonograph records
$ .29, $ .49 and $1.98

Green Duck Metal Stamping Co.
1520 W. Montana
Chicago, Illinois
Buttons — $ .02 ea.

Ideal Toy Corps.
184-10 Jamaica Avenue
Hollis, L. I., N. Y.
Vinyl Plastic Inflatable Toys
$4.00 and $7.00
Hand Puppets — $1.00

Lowe, Inc.
1324 - 52nd Street
Kenosha, Wisconsin
Coloring Books, Self Erasing Slate—$ .29

Phoenix Candy Co., Inc.
151 - 35th Street
Brooklyn 32, N. Y.
Candy Taffy Kisses — $ .05 per box

Nadel and Sons Corp.
900 Broadway
New York, New York
Nutty Putty — $ .49

The Van Dam Rubber Co., Inc.
1299 Jerome Avenue
New York 52, N. Y.
Toy Balloons — $ .29 per pkg.

L. M. Becker & Co.
Brillion, Wisconsin
Action rings and candy sticks — $ .05

Wilkening Manufacturing Co.
1000 S. 71st Street
Philadelphia 42, Pa.
Finger Puppets, Novelty Kazoo and
Walking Spring Toy — $1.00

Coral Records
445 Park Avenue
New York, New York
Record Albums — $3.00

Spec-Toy-Culars, Inc.
35-35 35th St.
Long Island City 6, N. Y.
Musical Toys — $1.00

The trade sheet above dates from the early '60s; names and prices may have changed.

STOOGE MANIA

THE RAREST OF THE RARE

Not all Stooges collectibles are available to anyone who has the price. Some items are, well, priceless, because they're one-of-a-kind personal items, even handmade. To get your hands on such items, be prepared to beg, borrow, steal, or drive to West Virginia. The items pictured here and on the next page are truly hard to find.

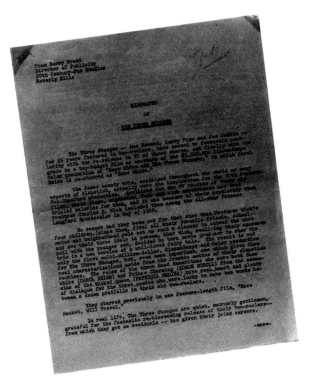

20th Century–Fox biography released to promote *Snow White and the Three Stooges* contains a complete account of the team's rise to fame, some of which is actually true. Such promotional items are extremely popular collectibles.

Shemp's cuff links—personal items such as these are considered the most valuable Stooges collectibles of all.

Moe Howard wrote on this letterhead on behalf of the "3 Stooges" in the early 1970s.

Even the Stooges themselves were movie fans. And, according to a 20th Century-Fox biography released in the early 1960s, the actor most admired by the Stooges was Spencer Tracy.

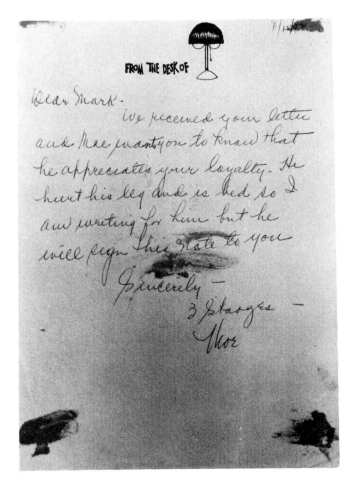

A fortunate (and well-connected) fan poses with the Stooges after a personal appearance by the team. The resulting snapshot remains a truly rare collectible.

As fan adulation mounted, some of the Stooges had special stationery printed. Larry Fine's incorporated artwork depicting his favorite activity—fiddling.

Stooges fan Erin Jacka poses with a doll made for her by Joe Besser. Joe, whose hobbies include repairing toys for neighborhood children, presented Erin with the doll as a gift in 1982.

#20

After Emil Sitka joined the Stooges in the 1970s, replacing Larry Fine, he wrote a story that he hoped might be developed as a brand-new Stooges feature. According to Sitka, he wrote a treatment in which Curly Joe DeRita would play—believe it or not—the world's first pregnant man! The movie never came to be, however, as the team broke up when Moe Howard fell ill.

THE ULTIMATE QUIZ

#71-100

THE ULTIMATE QUIZ FINAL PHASE—

71. Curly masquerades as a burly wrestler, Bustoff, in which Stooges short?

72. Which member of the Stooges never made a film appearance without his partners?

73. Which Stooges film has Curly playing both himself and his father?

74. Name the Stooges short in which Lloyd Bridges plays a man shouting into a telephone—his only appearance with the Stooges.

75. Which was the first of the Stooges shorts casting the Stooges as the Pip Boys?

76. Which Stooges short has Curly, Larry, and Moe searching for "an honest man," with disastrous results?

77. The Stooges spoof political conventions in which 1952 short subject?

78. Which Stooges short features "Bonanza's" Dan Blocker in a supporting role?

79. Who provides the voice of the radio announcer in the Stooges short *Dunked in the Deep* (1949)?

80. What is the title of the Stooges film in which the boys perform their classic vaudeville sketch "Niagara Falls"?

81. What is the name of the company the Stooges work for in their short subject *Muscle Up a Little Closer* (1957), written by veteran gagman Felix Adler?

82. What are the Stooges' phony names in their short subject *All the World's a Stooge* (1941), in which they disguise themselves as children?

83. What movie stuntman played the role of the Stooges' client, George B. Bopper, in their short subject *Spooks* (1953)?

The boys spend a break in the action wondering if they're in the right line of work.

84. Which classic Stooges short features the song "Swingin' the Alphabet"?

85. A future movie Tarzan costarred with the Stooges in their 1950 comedy *Punchy Cowpunchers.* What is his name?

86. Which Stooges comedy features old footage from Stooges shorts *A Plumbing We Will Go* (1940), *Half-Wits' Holiday* (1947), and *Vagabond Loafers* (1949)?

87. Which Stooges short was based on an idea conceived by Moe's wife, Helen Howard?

88. Who plays the role of the crazed movie producer in *Pardon My Clutch* (1948)?

89. Who plays the role of the train conductor in the Stooges' first starring film, *Woman Haters* (1934)?

90. Curly masquerades as an Indian maiden in which Stooges short?

91. Which Stooges film has the boys masquerading as Naki, Saki, and Whacki?

92. Which Stooges short has Moe playing the role of a psychiatrist, complete with German accent?

In the 1960s, Moe Howard tried to persuade Columbia Pictures to sell him rights to the Stooges short subjects for several million dollars. Columbia practically laughed him out of the office. And no wonder. The studio earned hundreds of millions of dollars from those old films, and the money continues to roll in. The Stooges themselves, however, each made less than half a million dollars, total, over a period of 24 years. Today, most major television stars earn more than that in *one* year.

93. Which Stooges short features Joe Besser with a head of hair, thanks to a neatly placed toupee?

94. Which late 1940s Stooge film has the boys being kidnapped to the mythical State of Anemia?

95. What is the name of Phil Van Zandt's mad scientist character in the Stooges' 3-D short subject *Spooks* (1953)?

96. What is the title of the Stooges comedy in which the boys parodied the classic western *High Noon* (1952)?

97. Which Stooges comedy finds the boys working as "Minute Menders"?

98. *Ants in the Pantry* (1936) features Bud Jamison as a pianist. What is the name of his character?

99. In *Three Little Pigskins* (1934), what numbers do the Stooges wear on their jerseys?

100. Complete the following motto: "One for all, all for one, _____!"

STILL SHOTS #7

What classic motion picture are these scenes from?
A. *Dial M for Moron*
B. *For Your Eyes Phonely*
C. *Rebels without a Dime*

APPENDIX

THE ULTIMATE QUIZ ANSWERS

HOW YOU RATE

If, after enduring all 100 questions, you still feel confident enough to compare your results with those of your cohorts, the following chart will help you judge the outcome.

Number Correct:

95–100   You are the ultimate Stooges fan. You're also a social outcast. (How else would you know so much about these guys?) Go outside and get some fresh air.

85–95   Your knowledge of the Stooges is admirable, and you, too, should seek some sort of outside activity. Too bad there's no cash prize here, huh?

70–85   You're not fanatical, but you've spent a lot of time in front of the tube. You'd still be the most knowledgeable Stooges authority at most parties, but that's really nothing to be ashamed of.

55–70   Chances are, you used to watch the Stooges a lot, but lately you're starting to slip. What'd you do—get married? In fact, you probably don't even remember Curly's real name anymore.

40–55   And you call yourself a Stooge fan. You've completely lost touch with hundreds of bits of information; stop whatever you're doing and head for the nearest television set.

25–40   You're new to this, aren't you? Better take notes from now on.

0–25   You'd rather be watching

Donahue, but somebody put you up to this. You're still not sure whether Curly is the one with the frizzy hair.

ULTIMATE QUIZ ANSWERS

1. Moella, Larrine, and Shempetta, played by the Stooges themselves.
2. *Whack*, whose slogan is "If it's a good picture, it's out of whack."
3. Nill, Null, and Void.
4. B. O. Pictures.
5. Fuller Rath.
6. The "Punjab Diamond," which he mistakes for an after-dinner mint.
7. Santa Claus suits.
8. Door-to-door greeting card salesmen.
9. Florabell, Corabell, and Dorabell, who jointly refuse to start the honeymoon until the house is built.
10. Ziller, Zeller, and Zoller, three eminent psychiatrists.
11. Ever Rest Pet Cemetery.
12. Hyden Zeke, played by Fred Kelsey.
13. J.O. Dunkfeather, played by William Kelly, who also narrates the short.
14. "The eel," a slippery criminal who disguises himself as a woman.
15. Nora, played by Babe London, complete with blacked-out teeth.
16. Frank Mitchell, who later became part of the "New Three Stooges" stage act.
17. Hotel Costa Plente.
18. Quff (pronounced "cuff").
19. A zoot suit, so he can impress the girls.
20. "The Original Two-Man Quartet."
21. President Ward Robe.
22. Percy Pomeroy, played by Stooges straight man Eddie Laughton.
23. The Amalgamated Association of Morons.
24. He doesn't eat duck; he's a vegetarian.
25. Ned Glass, an old family friend of Moe Howard.
26. Moehicus, Larrycus, and Curlycue.
27. Onion Oil Company, presided over by Fuller Grime (played by Stanley Blystone).
28. Rhum Boogie, which is inhabited by cannibals.
29. Moe Howard, complete with white beard and flowing white hair.
30. Brighto, which the boys first mistake for car polish.
31. Buffalo Billious, Will Bill Hiccup, and Just Plain Bill.
32. Transylvania Railroad Company.
33. A pet store owner who bills himself as "Larry, your pet man."
34. Queen Hotsytotsy.
35. Dr. Dippy's Retreat.
36. Seven hours.
37. Moe in Germany, Larry in Italy, and Shemp in France.
38. Like Adolf Hitler, he is a paperhanger.
39. Walter Brennan.
40. The Great Svengarlic.
41. Los Arms Hospital.
42. Lightning Pest Control, presided over by Mr. Mouser.
43. "Home on the Range," which they sing while perched atop a kitchen stove.
44. $6 million.
45. Helen Blazes.
46. Sunev, which is Venus spelled backward.
47. *Cash and Carry* (1937). He was Jimmy, a crippled boy whom the Stooges try to assist.
48. Monty Collins, who also cowrote the film with Elwood Ullman.
49. Mildew Girl's College.
50. Cess, Poole, and Drayne, with Emil Sitka as Mr. Poole.
51. F.B. Eye.
52. Roquefort, Camembert, and Limburger.
53. *Pop Goes the Easel* (1935).
54. *Oil's Well That Ends Well* (1958).
55. Emil Sitka.
56. *Cuckoo on a Choo Choo* (1952).
57. Moe Howard.
58. *Spooks* (1953).
59. The Acme Exterminating Company.
60. Omay.
61. Wild Hyacinth perfume.
62. *Punch Drunks* (1935).
63. Curly Howard.
64. *Fiddlers Three* (1948).
65. Mr. Heller.
66. *Three Hams on Rye* (1950).
67. *Pest Man Wins* (1951).

The Stooges prepare to "make a wish" with an unfortunate fan.

68. Joe Besser.
69. *Three Little Pigskins* (1934).
70. *Pop Goes the Easel* (1935).
71. *Grips, Grunts, and Groans* (1937).
72. Larry Fine.
73. *Three Dumb Clucks* (1937).
74. *They Stooge to Conga* (1943).
75. *Sing a Song of Six Pants* (1947).
76. *So Long, Mr. Chumps* (1941).
77. *Three Dark Horses* (1952).
78. *Outer Space Jitters* (1957).
79. Moe Howard.
80. *Gents without Cents* (1944).
81. Adler & Company.
82. Frankie (Curly), Mabel (Larry), and Johnny (Moe).
83. Frank Mitchell, who later played the "Moe" role in a stage act called "The New Three Stooges."
84. *Violent Is the Word for Curly* (1938).
85. Jock Mahoney.
86. *Scheming Schemers* (1956), filmed after Shemp Howard's death but featuring the "Shemp" character through use of old footage.
87. *Hoi Polloi* (1935).
88. Emil Sitka.
89. Walter Brennan, who, according to Moe Howard, had trouble remembering his lines.
90. *Whoops I'm an Indian* (1936).
91. *No Dough, Boys* (1944), in which they impersonate a trio of Japanese wrestlers.
92. *Sweet and Hot* (1958), in which Moe temporarily abandons his trademark sugar-bowl haircut.
93. *Fifi Blows Her Top* (1958).
94. *Fuelin' Around* (1949).
95. Dr. Jekyll. His assistant is named Mr. Hyde.
96. *Shot in the Frontier* (1954).
97. *How High Is Up?* (1940).
98. Professor Repulso.
99. H_2O,?, and 6-7/8.
100. ". . . every man for himself!"

ANSWERS TO CHARACTERISTIC QUOTES #1-18

1. Larry in *Micro-Phonies*, 1945
2. Moe in *Spook Louder*, 1943
3. Moe in *He Cooked His Goose*, 1952
4. Curly in *Busy Buddies*, 1944

Larry sneaks a cigarette during a break in the filming of *Gold Raiders*. Note the script in Moe's left hand.

5. Curly in *Oily to Bed, Oily to Rise*, 1939
6. Larry in *Hold That Lion*, 1947
7. Larry in *Pardon My Clutch*, 1948
8. Curly in *Dizzy Detectives*, 1944
9. Curly in *So Long, Mr. Chumps*, 1941
10. Moe in *Crash Goes the Hash*, 1944
11. Moe in *Booty and the Beast*, 1953
12. Larry in *The Tooth Will Out*, 1951
13. Larry in *Crash Goes the Hash*, 1944
14. Curly in *We Want Our Mummy*, 1939
15. Larry in *An Ache in Every Stake*, 1941
16. Moe in *Listen, Judge*, 1952
17. Curly in *Movie Maniacs*, 1936
18. Moe in *If a Body Meets a Body*, 1946

ANSWERS TO STOOGESEARCH PUZZLE

The following titles can be found within the puzzle, whether read across, diagonally, up and down, or backward:

- Punch Drunks
- Slippery Silks
- Spooks
- Hot Ice
- Who Done It
- Creeps
- Hokus Pokus
- Gents in a Jam
- Kook's Tour
- Restless Knights
- Boobs in Arms
- Out West
- Fright Night
- Pals and Gals
- Matri-Phony
- Fiddlers Three
- Hot Scots
- Quiz Whiz
- Hot Stuff

ANSWERS TO STOOGES CROSSWITS PUZZLE

ACROSS

1. Knucklehead
7. Moron
8. Moe
9. JB
10. Sap
12. Idiot
13. Stupe
15. Slap
16. Dumbbells
17. JD
19. Porcupine
23. Nitwit
24. Hotsy
29. Larry Fine
33. Twists

DOWN

2. Numbskull
3. Lunk
4. Halfwit
5. Dimwit
6. Joe
11. Birdbrain
13. SH
14. *Gents*
18. Dunce
20. IH
21. *No*
22. ET
25. Ted
26. Curly
27. Fifi
28. Stooge
30. Ant
31. Fat
32. *Nut*

The Three Stooges, 1960s-style, make a hasty exit after a rousing personal appearance. Note the tight security that surrounded the team even then.

WHERE TO GET IT

Following is a list of dealers, companies, and kindly curators who may be of some assistance in locating Stooge memorabilia and products.

CALIFORNIA

BUDGET VIDEO
4590 Santa Monica Blvd.
Los Angeles, CA 90029

COLUMBIA PICTURES HOME ENTERTAINMENT
2901 W. Alamedia Ave.
Burbank, CA 91505

DISCOUNT VIDEO TAPES, INC.
1117 No. Hollywood Way
PO Box 7122
Burbank, CA 91510

EDDIE BRANDT'S SATURDAY MATINEE
PO Box 3232
North Hollywood, CA 91609

LOS ANGELES BUTTON COMPANY
845 W. Washington Blvd.
Los Angeles, CA 90015

OPERATOR THIRTEEN VIDEO
PO Box 15602
Los Angeles, CA 91615

RHINO RECORDS, INC.
1201 Olympic Blvd.
Santa Monica, CA 90404

COLORADO

UPTOWN RUBBER STAMP
159 Mountain Ave.
Fort Collins, CO 80521

ILLINOIS

LIBER-TEE'S, INC.
PO Box 25878
Chicago, IL 60625

MYLSTAR ELECTRONICS, INC.
165 W. Lake Rd.
Northlake, IL 60164

KENTUCKY

UNION UNDERWEAR COMPANY, INC.
1 Fruit of the Loom Dr.
Bowling Green, KY 42101

MAINE

THS COMPANIES
1-3 Union St.
Dover Foxcraft, ME 04426

MICHIGAN

ARTWEAR
969 S. Hunter
Birmingham, MI 48011

THE BUTTON UP COMPANY
195 W. Nine Mile Rd., Suite 216
Ferndale, MI 48220

CLASSIC MOVIE AND COMIC CENTER
19047 Middlebelt
Livonia, MI Mid-7 Shopping Center 48152

MISSOURI

HEFFALUMPS OF ST. LOUIS
26 Maryland Plaza
St. Louis, MO 63108

NEW YORK

BEN COOPER
33 34th St.
Brooklyn, NY 11232

BENAY ALBEE NOVELTY COMPANY, INC.
52-01 Flushing Ave.
Maspeth, NY 11378

CRABWALK, INC.
648 Broadway
New York, NY 10012

JERRY OHLINGER'S MOVIE MATERIAL STORE
120 West Third St.
New York, NY 10012

LUDLOW SALES CORPORATION
PO Box 554
Chelsea Station, NY 10011

THE MANUSCRIPT SOCIETY, UNIVERSAL AUTOGRAPH
COLLECTOR'S CLUB
Box 467
Rockville Center, NY 11576-0467

PLAYMORE INC. PUBLISHERS/WALDMAN PUBLISHING
CORPORATION
18 E. 41st St.
New York, NY 10012

OHIO

VIDEO CONNECTION
3240 Sylvania Ave.
Toledo, OH 43613

PENNSYLVANIA

BRIGHT IDEAS, INC.
300 N. Pottstown Pick
Exton, PA 19341

GERARD ENTERPRISES
253 Carry Holly Rd. Suite K
Pleasant Hills, PA 15236

TEXAS

REMEMBER WHEN
2431 Valwood Parkway
Dallas, TX 75234

WASHINGTON

GASOLINE ALLEY ANTIQUES
6501-20th N.E.
Seattle, WA 98115

WISCONSIN

THE CARD COACH
PO Box 122-S
Plover, WI 54467